THE CORRUPTION
OF
MOSLEM MINDS

THE CORRUPTION
OF
MOSLEM MINDS

DR. NADER POURHASSAN

BARBED WIRE
PUBLISHING
LAS CRUCES, NEW MEXICO

First printing: June 2002. Printed in the United States of America.
Second printing, October 2002. Printed in Hong Kong, PRC.

ISBN #0-9711930-7-X

DEDICATION

This book is dedicated to a woman whose Christian love opened my eyes to the hatred that I had been taught by my culture—hatred for non-Moslems and for anyone who didn't agree with my way of seeing the world. I learned from her that Jesus was right when he told us that God wants us all to love each other unconditionally, and that only love can destroy the hatred that maintains the world in its divided state. Cris, this is for you.

Special thanks also to my son whose constant pleas to play football have delayed the publication of this book for seven years.

This book is also dedicated to my father who passed away a few years ago. If he had not made so many sacrifices to send me to the United States for my education, I would never have accomplished anything. And also to my mother, who has cared for and loved me unconditionally my whole life. I love you, Mom.

I would also like to extend my thanks to my older brother, Amir, who encouraged me tremendously in writing this book and was a real guidance to me throughout my life. I always looked up to you, Amir.

Nader Pourhassan
March, 2002

TABLE OF CONTENTS

PREFACE

This book is the result of my personal disillusionment with Islam as it is manifested in the modern world. The message of the Koran is resoundingly simple. We should believe in God, which of itself would encourage us to be good, and love our neighbor. If we do, we will go to Heaven: "Those who do good to men or women and have faith [in God], we will give them life, a pure life, and their reward will be greater than their actions."[1]

This message, which is stated clearly over sixty times in the Koran, has been perverted by those who seek to promote themselves as spiritual leaders, with appalling results—most shockingly, the attacks on America on September 11th, 2001.

Seven years ago, my growing cynicism about the form which contemporary Islam takes prompted me to start researching Islam, and I turned to the original text of the Koran for the first time. My sense of disillusionment with everything I had been taught to believe as true about Islam grew as I learned about the disparity between the holy book and Islam as it is practiced today. Now, more than ever, there is an urgent need for Moslems and non-Moslems alike to understand the truth about Islam, and to return to the original message of the Prophet Muhammad, and that of Jesus—that humankind should strive to be good, to love God and one another—and to recognize the common background of the three religious faiths that dominate the world stage today: Judaism, Christianity and Islam. Only when we stand together will we be able to discard the burden of history and move towards a brighter future.

There is more than one edition of the Koran, and the numbering of the verses varies slightly from one edition to the next. People wishing to check my references against their copy of the Koran might find that there are some discrepancies, unless they are working from the same edition. For the sake of clarity, I'd like to stress that the edition I used was translated from Arabic to Persian by Mesbah Zadeh, under the patronage of Muhammad Ali Elmi, and published by Afset. The English translation was provided by Anwar, a CD containing the Koran translated into

English, from a variety of sources. Citations take the form of two sets of numbers. For example 2:17 means "chapter two, verse seventeen," with 17 appearing in the original at the beginning of the verse rather than at the end. Where the Bible is quoted, I have used the New King James version. Please note that the terms "Torah" and "Old Testament" are interchangeable, while I most commonly use the word "Bible" to refer to the New Testament.

My family background is Shiite, and my greater knowledge of this religious tradition (as opposed to the Sunni, the other major Moslem group) is reflected throughout the book.

INTRODUCTION

I was born in 1963 in Tehran, the capital of Iran. My father was serving in the Iranian Army Aviation Force at that time. Himself the product of a marriage between a gentle, caring mother and a sadistic father, he treated his children rather brutally. My elder brother Amir and I were often beaten—sometimes because we'd misbehaved, but more often for no reason at all. It was not until I reached adulthood that my father and I developed a healthy, respectful relationship.

The Iran of my childhood was largely populated by people who had received little formal education. It was also a time of political and cultural strife, with the Shah battling for power against the religious leader, Ayatollah Khomeni. The events that occurred throughout the 1960s and 70s were to shape the Middle East for many years. Their effects are still felt today, as the Cold War between the Soviet Union and the United States is replaced by a new threat—the simmering conflict between the Islamic nations and, effectively, the rest of the world.

By the time I was fourteen years old, my father had been in the United States for training four times. He was a high achiever, often excelling far beyond what was normally expected of Army Aviation officers in the time of the Shah. As a result, he had spent long stretches—as much as two years at a time—in American universities. Because of his experience, he decided that Amir and I should be educated in the United States. The news that we were going to America was not met with delight by the other members of the family. My mother and grandmother—and, in fact, their entire family—were devout Moslems, and had strong anti-American feelings. They were worried about the negative influence that Americans would surely have on our development. Now, these were kind, gentle women whose kindness had made my childhood with a violent father tolerable. It is not difficult to understand why I respected their opinion, and assumed that their prejudices were correct.

Just before Amir and I left Iran in 1979, our grandmother said, "My dear grandsons, I say goodbye to you with a very heavy heart. Please take care of yourselves in the United States, because it is a very bad country.

The people there are Christians, and the most impure people there are. If they touch you, make sure you wash your hands, because Christians are impure in the eyes of God."

I loved my grandmother very much, and these words affected me deeply. I promised her that I'd do my best to stay away from those dirty Christians.

Our boarding school was in the small, deeply religious Christian town of Searcy, Arkansas. My mother accompanied us on the trip, which was a great expense for the family. She was worried about us, and concerned that we would be vulnerable and unprotected when she left. She was also trying to limit expenses, as there was barely enough money to pay for one year's tuition. We were welcomed by the superintendent of the school who, when he realized that we had nowhere to stay, took us into his home rather than direct us to the nearest cheap motel. There we stayed until term began. I was very impressed by his kindness and hospitality.

"These must be the best Moslems I've ever met!" I exclaimed to my mother.

You can imagine how surprised I was to learn that they were Christians. "But Grandma said... ," I started to complain.

Mom interrupted me and told me that these people were the exception to the rule. It was clear that there was no more to say on the matter so I kept my thoughts to myself.

The contrast between the things that I had been taught to believe about America and the kindness I received from so many Americans confused me. Despite having been taught to hate America and the Americans, I loved being there, and enjoyed the company of Americans. The other students were friendly, the school offered wonderful athletic facilities and the establishment's rules ensured the harmonious functioning of the institution. Even the air, it seemed, was more fragrant than in Iran.

During my time at the school, I grew close to both the superintendent and the principal. The principal, Mr. Dilles, was a devout Christian and tried to convert me to his faith. Although I responded politely, his efforts always make me laugh inside. Convert? Never! But a few years later I discovered that Amir had been through a secret baptism. This news had been kept from me, as everyone knew how strongly I felt about Islam, and feared an angry reaction. They were right. When the news was leaked to me, I was distraught. I searched the campus for Amir and, when I finally found him, asked if the rumor I'd heard was true.

"Did you change your religion?" I demanded to know.

"No, I haven't," he answered.

I was still unconvinced. I slapped his face, and told him to slap me back if he was still a Moslem. He turned the other cheek. Breaking into tears, I slapped him again, crying out, "How could you do this to our family? You will break our grandmother's heart!"

I had never been so depressed and angry before. I complained to God: "I am so angry with you! If Islam is right, why do these Christians feel so good when they're at church? They're supposed to be impure and evil! Why do I keep meeting so many good Christians?"

After two years in the United States, I still hadn't met any evil people, and this frustrated me. Everyone likes to have their prejudices confirmed, and I was no exception.

1979 was the year that Amir and I moved to the United States to study, and it was also a year of momentous events in the history of Iran. After many years of struggling against the Shah of Iran, Ayatollah Mousavei Khomeni had finally overcome his regime. Iranian loyalties were divided, and many different groups were formed, each with its own separate ideology. I favored the followers of Khomeni, and decided to support them with all my heart and soul. Young and easily swayed, I studied martial arts and eventually earned a black belt, believing that somehow this would aid me in helping to fight for Iran. I even abandoned my studies in America, to join Iran in the war against Iraq. However, shortly after I visited the front line and observed the war for two weeks, my family demanded I return to the United States instead of joining the fighters, as I had intended. A number of religious leaders backed up my parents' stance, telling me that I should return and complete my education in America. They convinced me that in order for me to help Iran fight against the "Great Satan," I needed to get an education from the Americans first. I believed that, as I was paying higher tuition fees than American citizens, I didn't owe the United States anything, and I returned. At that time I was living in Utah, a state whose strict religious ethical system, although very different to that of the Islamic countries, also dominates the culture at every level.

After graduating from Utah State University with a degree in mechanical engineering, I enrolled at Brigham Young University in a masters program—again, a highly religious school where the prevailing ethical system was very different to my own. By now, my whole family—all of whom were staunch supporters of Khomeni's regime—was living in the United States, while continuing to hold onto their distaste for the American way of life. I enjoyed my time at the university although, for years, I observed all of the obligatory rites regarding purification after contact with a Christian. Prejudice aside, I fell in love with a Catholic American woman whom I met while studying for my masters degree. My parents were less than impressed with the choice of my heart.

"Take her as a girlfriend to quench your lust," was Mom's advice, "and later I'll find you a real woman in Iran to be your wife." She refused to believe that the American woman I fell in love with did not believe in sexual relations before marriage. In fact, no American woman could be pure in her eyes. Her idea of a "real" woman was someone who would keep herself covered from head to toe, and observe all the "rules of Islam" as they are interpreted by Moslem religious leaders.

I was not at all happy at the prospect of my mother choosing a godly woman for me, and proposed marriage to the woman I loved. One day, I told Mom that I had a surprise for her, and asked my wife to show her the ring I'd given her. I believed that as soon as Mom saw how much I loved my wife, she would learn to love her too. Instead, she forced a pained smile and asked, "Did you actually marry her, or did you just buy her a ring?" I assured her that the marriage was genuine.

"You said you loved Islam and your country," Mom wailed, "and then you turn around and marry an American soldier!" (My wife was in the Army National Guard.)

As you can imagine, my marriage did not get off to a wonderful start, and the conflict between my parents and me didn't abate. Dad would joke about how American women always cheat on their husbands, and Mom kept insisting that my new wife was evil just because she was not a Moslem. Even when I assured Mom that my wife believed in God and, in fact, attended church, she laughed bitterly and said that Christians were impure, and had no place in God's kingdom.

However, I can't blame other people for all the difficulties that Cris and I faced as a married couple. I found it difficult to accept that my wife wanted to wear make-up, and to dress according to Christian standards of modesty rather than my own, which I believed were also God's. I started to nag her, until things reached the point whereby she was in constant fear of criticism. I was torn between the message of a culture that assured me that I was not a real man if I allowed my wife to live any way other than according to Islamic law, and the desire to make the marriage work.

Around this time, I attended an Islamic meeting in Utah given by a religious leader appointed by the Iranian government to promote cohesion among the various Islamic communities in the United States. After listening to what was a very typical speech, the floor was open to questions. One member of the audience asked, "Can a Moslem man allow his wife to wear make-up?"

The answer came immediately: "Many years ago, a famous religious leader said that those men who allow their wives to wear make-up should be known as 'pimps', because they are supplying society with prostitutes. God does not love pimps and will have nothing to do with them."

Again, I was torn between two conflicting reactions. On the one hand, I hated the speaker for saying such things, and on the other, I wanted more than ever before for my wife to stop using make-up. At home, I presented her with an ultimatum: "From now on, I don't want to see any make-up on your face!"

She argued back: "Why do you shave and make yourself presentable? Is there something wrong with you, or do you just want to feel good about yourself?"

"That's different," I retorted, "this is the way things are. It's fine for me to make myself look good, but it's not acceptable for you. You can just choose what you want—to be with me and agree with my rules, or to do what you want, and be alone."

By now, we had a child, and I figured that I could make my wife penniless and homeless without my support. I thought that this would coerce her into submitting to my will—to follow God's path and embrace the truth of Islam. But I was wrong.

"I've had enough of you and your religion," she said, "I'm leaving."

I was horrified! It had never occurred to me that she might really go. "Don't leave right away," I urged, "let me just check that the Koran really says you can't wear make-up so that I can be sure I'm doing the right thing." I suppose that even then I suspected deep down that I might be blindly following the dictates of religious leaders without caring about the original laws of God. And so I began to do something that I had never done before. I began to read the Koran.

It didn't take me very long to realize that the message the Koran contains is the same beautiful message recorded in the Christian Bible—that given to Moses in the Old Testament (the Torah) and Jesus in the New Testament. It has nothing to do with the nonsense to which so many modern Moslems subscribe. This revelation opened my eyes. I started reading the Koran for literally hours every day, studying the real laws of Islam as they were recorded fourteen centuries ago, when the Arabs were still a pastoral people sharing the deserts of the Middle East with the Jews and other related peoples. The Koran is the most holy of books for a Moslem, and yet the rules for living prescribed by it have nothing at all to do with modern Moslem laws.

Every Friday night at the Islamic religious center I attended, volunteers were invited to give speeches. When my turn came, I asked if anyone in the room had read the Koran in translation.[1] No one had. In any case, I asked, "Are the women here aware that there is no law anywhere in the Koran obliging women to cover their hair or dress as modestly as they do?" In fact, I told them, the Koran's instructions about dress seem consistent with those indicated in the Christian Bible.

The women at the meeting were shocked, but not ready to accept that the oppression that they had been tolerating for their entire lives had nothing to do with the word of God. Surprisingly, some of the most fanatical adherents of the often insane laws espoused by Moslem religious leaders are the very women who suffer the most under the belief system. Nobody likes to hear that they have gone to a great deal of trouble for no reason!

As my studies of the Koran progressed, my conviction that the way Islam is practiced today has nothing in common with Muhammad's teachings grew. Initially, I searched desperately for confirmation that the laws I had been taught my whole life were indeed the same ones given to Muhammad by God. Instead, I reached the conclusion that they were drastically—unrecognizably—different. That the Islamic laws which had been branded into my soul since childhood were no more than the handiwork of men whose mission it was to advance their own power. It is for this reason that so many Moslem people in the world live in misery and suffer under barbaric systems of government and justice while their nations fail to develop economically.

This realization represented a dramatic shift in my world view. Before, I had believed that the way Moslems lived was the only true and godly way to live. I believed the doctrine my countrymen and women had taught me—that the Moslems were God's favored people. But I had never asked myself why, if this was true, so many Moslem countries did nothing to protect their people from human rights abuses; why the oppression of women was widespread and officially endorsed; why, despite a long heritage of Arab learning and culture and lands rich in natural resources, so many Moslem nations remained impoverished. Is this how God treats His chosen people? Is this how He believes advantage to be? It made no sense. Instead, the lesson I learned was the truth of Karl Marx's famous observation, that religion is the "opium of the masses," making them at once complacent and miserable, resigned and resentful. Present-day Islam has done nothing for its people but prolong their ignorance, their poverty and their lack of anything approaching human rights. As a Moslem, I know from my own experience that religious Moslems put all their faith in their spiritual leaders. They believe what they are told, and those who dare to argue are immediately considered to be corrupt nonbelievers. Similar trends can be observed in Judaism and Christianity.

My own crisis of faith resulted in my becoming deeply familiar with the Koran and the messages it contains. My frustration at the difference between the Koran's teachings and the way most Moslems live today has been the impetus behind researching and writing this book after years of study of the original texts. Whether you are a Moslem or non-Moslem, a Christian, a Jew, a Hindu or indeed of any faith, I hope that you will find my comments enlightening, and be inspired to read the Koran for yourself. The only way that we can break the current impasse between the Moslem and the non-Moslem peoples is by fostering mutual understanding of the many historical, cultural and religious ties that bind us.

Chapter 1

THE HISTORY OF ISLAM

The term "Islam" derives from the three-letter Arabic root s-l-m, which generates words with interrelated meanings, including "surrender," "submission," "commitment" and "peace." Commonly, Islam refers to the monotheistic religion revealed to Muhammad bin (son of) Abdullah between 610 and 632 A. D. The name "Islam" was instituted by the Koran, the sacred scripture revealed to the Prophet Muhammad. For believers, Islam is not a new religion nor a complement to the achievements of Judaism and Christianity. Rather, it represents the final and absolute reiteration of the primordial message of God's oneness, a theme found in earlier monotheistic religious traditions. It is, they believe, the final step in an evolutionary chain of religions, preceded by Christianity and Judaism and superior to both.

Although Islam is a religion, it should also be viewed by its adherents in much broader terms. What many, both within and outside Islam, would see as manifestations of the teachings of the Koran—such as the excessive modesty of women or the complex rules regarding washing—are actually examples of a culture's ethnic peculiarities. Most cultural behaviors in Islamic countries have no correspondence in the Koran and are the product of a tradition propagated largely by religious leaders with the intention of keeping their people subdued, ignorant and easily manipulated. But before denouncing the practices of unscrupulous religious leaders, let's take a look at the origins of the true Islam.

The Prophet Muhammad was born in Mecca in 571 and orphaned at an early age. Cared for by his grandfather and his uncle throughout his childhood, he grew up to marry Khadijeh, his first wife, when he was twenty-five years old. She was forty years old, and had been divorced twice. Khadijeh was to become a very holy woman of Islam in the eyes of the Moslem people, especially the Shiite.

Muhammad was appointed by God to be a prophet in 610 when he was forty years old[1], and the message of the Koran was revealed to him over a period of twenty-three years, the first thirteen of which he spent in Mecca, and the last ten in Medina. Mecca, in what is now Saudi Arabia, remains the most important site of pilgrimage for Moslems all over the world. Muhammad's message was immediately opposed by the idol worshippers of Mecca, who saw him as a threat to their customs and traditions. He and his followers were forced to flee in fear of their lives. God spoke to Muhammad, telling him to seek shelter from a Christian king, named Najashi[2]. The shelter was given, and the actions of this king saved Muhammad, his followers and the newly born faith of Islam from an early and immediate extinction.

Many subsequent attempts were made to kill the prophet and his followers. Wars raged, but no attempt was successful. Islam spread across the region with astonishing rapidity, and was present in three continents within five decades of the prophet's death. In the early days of Islam's growth as an organized religion, missionary efforts were directed towards non-believers or idolaters rather than Jews or Christians, who were recognized as believers.

The teachings of the Koran are the revelations received by Muhammad from God, and it confirms those formerly taught by Moses and later Jesus Christ. Many of the prophets mentioned in the Koran are the same as those of the Old Testament, including Noah, Job, Jonah, Solomon, David, Joseph, Jacob, Isaiah, Ishmael, Lot and many more. Some of the events involving the lives of Moses and Jesus and their followers have also been accounted for. Although Islam shares a great deal of common ground with Judaism and Christianity, Muhammad's teachings were the result of his prophethood, and the revelations directly received by him from God.

When the prophet's wife Khadijeh died, Muhammad remarried—not once, but many times. For this reason, many Moslems believe that polygamy is still acceptable in contemporary societies. However, the teaching in the Koran about plural marriage refers to special circumstances. Plural marriage was recommended at that time as a manner in which orphans and widows could be cared for when all the men of a tribe had been exterminated—plural marriage was not commended per se, but only to facilitate the care of children left fatherless: "Give orphans their property and do not substitute something worthless for something good, nor swallow up their wealth along with your own wealth. This would be a great outrage. If you are afraid you will not deal fairly with orphans, then marry such women [widows] as seem good to you, two or three or four. If you fear you will not act justly, then marry one woman only, or as many as you are capable of without committing an injustice."[3]

Only when many widows and orphans were left with no one to provide for them, was it suggested that polygamy was acceptable.

Muhammad's wives varied widely in age, including at least one of advanced years. His marriages were political, and not based on desire or other personal reasons. By marrying many women, Muhammad united tribes which had previously been enemies. At that time, tribal alliances were often made, and peace treaties sealed, by means of marriage contracts. Muhammad's example has often been cited as justification for polygamy and spousal abuse, but this is a false extrapolation. The Koran says that, in ordinary marriage, no man can be fair to more than one wife, and that monogamy is the ideal.[4] Non-Moslems have sometimes condemned Muhammad for having many wives. But we must consider everything in the context of its time and fully understand the social and cultural environment of any given era before casting judgment.

Much has been made of the instructions given to Muhammad's wives in the Koran. Most religious leaders assume that these strict rules of conduct should be applied to the general population of Moslem women. This is a fallacy: Muhammad's wives were not just wives—they were also early political ambassadors uniting the various Arab tribes which had converted to Islam. For this reason, special rules of conduct applied to them, only to them and certainly not to other Moslem women. (This topic will be discussed in more detail in chapter six.)

Muhammad died at the age of sixty-three, of natural causes. The split of Islam into two distinct and mutually antagonistic groups—the Shiite and the Sunni—was immediate.

Ali, who later became the first *imam*[5] of the Shiite, was only a child when he became the first person to accept Muhammad's plea that all believers should follow the same God. He was Muhammad's cousin, and married to the prophet's youngest daughter Fatima, who is the most venerated female figure of Islamic tradition. They had two surviving sons, Hassan and Hussein, also considered to be *imams*. Shiite Moslems award ultimate powers to twelve *imams* as well as the prophet Muhammad and his daughter Fatima. However, they especially praise five people: Muhammad, Ali, Fatima, Hassan and Hussein. They pray to them to ask them to intercede with God on their behalf, calling them "Panjtan," which can be loosely translated as "the five persons."

But how, exactly, was Islam divided into two conflicting groups? After the Prophet Muhammad died in 632, some followers believed that Ali should be the leader of the Moslems, saying that he had been appointed by the prophet as successor. These people became Shiite. Those who became Sunni agree that Ali was appointed successor. However, at the time of Muhammad's death, they said that he was too young, so they insisted that he be preceded by three other followers, all of whom died prior to the leadership of Ali. These were: Abu Bakr, a friend of the prophet and the first adult male to embrace Islam, Umar, who ordered the protection of Christian sites in Jerusalem, and Uthman, who was responsible for having the Koran copied and dispersed throughout the Islamic world. Uthman was finally succeeded by Ali.

The contemporary Moslem world remains divided between the Shiite and the Sunni faiths. Eleven generations of men descended from Ali are very revered by Shiite Moslems, to the extent of being recognized as saints. Together with Ali, they are considered to be the twelve apostles of Muhammad.

Shiite people demonstrate their disrespect for the Sunni by manifesting their disdain of their three traditional leaders. Shiite religious leaders insist upon opposing those of the Sunni, in order to make their followers as different as possible. For example, they tell their followers to pray to God with their hands open, at either side, while the Sunnis pray with their hands closed. Shiite have also added a part to their prayer, called *ghonout*, which differs from that of the Sunni. Many other details of the Shiite faith are very different to those of the Sunni. For example, they cannot eat meat killed by anyone who hates the twelve *imams* of Shiite tradition, regardless of their faith, and the formalized washing they observe before prayer is very different to that of the Sunni. All of this despite the fact that in the Koran it states clearly that Moslems should strive to maintain unity. Not to do so, the Koran says, is worse than committing murder: "…persecution is more severe than slaughter."[6]

However, although less than 10% of all Moslems are Shiite, Shiites demand that the Sunni should change their ways and join them in order to maintain unity. On the other hand, some branches of Sunni consider the Shiite to be worse than atheists. This has caused a lot of tension. Hatred between the groups is fuelled constantly by the religious leaders of both and is an important contributing factor to the ongoing political and economic instability in the Middle East.

Shiite Moslems follow their religious leaders blindly, and these leaders insist upon obedience to a multitude of complex rules and guidelines which govern daily life. Today, many Iraqis and the vast majority of Iranians are Shiite. In other largely Moslem nations, most Moslems are Sunni and a small percentage are Shiite. These include Saudi Arabia, India (where Islam is a minority religion), Pakistan, (which split from India after independence from the British and is predominantly Moslem), and certain African and Far Eastern countries such as Malaysia. The influence of Islam on the socio-economic development of these countries, their relationships with other nations and the status of human and especially women's rights has been considerable. Moslem minorities are also present in a wide range of countries, including the United States, the United Kingdom and many, if not all, European nations where Moslems comprise a small percentage of the total population.

Chapter 2

THE THREE GREAT RELIGIONS

Judaism, Christianity and Islam have become increasingly detached from their common heritage. Many contemporary adherents of these faiths have little knowledge of the background they share—the prophets and the great degree of overlap and continuity between their most sacred texts—that make these three traditions all "branches on the same tree." Islam, Judaism, and Christianity all proclaim as their central message that one must worship the one God—variously referred to as God, Yahweh, Jehovah, Allah[1] and more—and do all the good one can during one's lifetime so as to receive one's eternal reward on the day of judgment:

"This group will inherit. They will inherit Heaven, and will be in it eternally."[2]

This simple idea is supposed to ensure that human beings live in harmony and love. Each time a new prophet appeared throughout the course of history, his message was supposed to strengthen the idea that we should all worship the one true God, rather than idols. If religious leaders of the three great faiths were less blind and narrow-minded, the commonality of these three religions would be a unifying factor, not a divisive one. The constant, ongoing conflict between the adherents of these faiths in the Middle East and elsewhere is fuelled by ignorance and the corruption of God's original message by self-serving religious leaders.

History relates the origins of monotheistic worship among earlier populations, as well as the original, unvarnished intentions of the prophets. These men appeared at different points in time, often uniting believers during their lives, only for division and conflict to reappear when they died. In the beginning, the idea that there was only one God divided humans into two categories—those who agreed with this, and those who did not. In short, believers and non-believers. With the appearance of each new prophet, the group of believers, rather than grow-ing in numbers and unity, began to split into conflicting groups. Why? Because, as long as there was no charismatic figure preaching love and togetherness, religious leaders cultivated personal power and their own images and manipulated their flocks to line their own pockets. They turned their particular group of believers into a money-making organiza-tion with themselves at the helm.

As time passed, the number of splinter groups of "true believers" pro-liferated until there were so many that the task of uniting them became almost impossible. For example, Jesus had to fight the ethos of those who did not believe in God, just as his forefather Abraham had done. But that wasn't all. He also had to fight the large number of Jews who believed in one God, but were reluctant to recognize a new prophet. Why? Because their religious leaders did not want to relinquish the reins of power. They had no reason to support a new voice preaching humility and compas-sion, and had every reason to fight it. They knew that their rules were rules of man and not of God and, knowing this, feared exposure for the char-latans they were.

Later, the prophet Muhammad was also fiercely opposed by Jewish and Christian religious leaders. His reiteration of God's message of peace and love was a new threat to the complacency of established powers. Today, Moslems who truly wish to follow the teachings of the Koran are rigorously rejected by Moslem religious leaders and their ignorant fol-lowers.

As recent events have shown, many Moslems are prepared to fight against the United States, believing it to be the enemy of God. But there is nothing godly at all about their own countries and societies! Instead, many Moslem religious leaders order the mass killing of innocent peo-ple—terrorism, in a word—and do this *in the name of God*. All of this despite the fact that the Koran strictly prohibits the taking of innocent life:

"...do not kill one another, God has been merciful towards you."[3]

Moslem religious leaders represent the Koran to their followers in a manner that could never be accepted by an educated person in his or her right mind. How easy it is to overlook the fact that the Koran brings us the same message as the Bible and the Torah: Believe in one God with all your heart and all your mind and do good in the land of God before you die. And for doing that, you will not only be rewarded with a piece of Heaven, but, more importantly, God will be happy with you.

This simple message from God reverberates, unchanging, throughout history. However, the destruction of God's laws in the hands of religious leaders corrupts it beyond recognition. Their personal ideals start to intrude into the laws of God, either when they actually change His holy book, or when they interpret its message in the manner that suits them best. Why? I believe that these are the key reasons:

First, religious leaders become very sensitive towards the differences between the various branches of their own religion, or the religions that preceded them. In order to forge a completely separate identity for themselves and their followers, they construct laws to make their group differ from others as much as possible. This occurs even at the expense of the true laws of God.

Second, subsequent religious leaders want to maintain the popularity they enjoy with their own group, and be seen to advance it. This is why, even if they can see that the religious rules are in conflict with the rules of God, they continue to follow them.

Third, as the circle of leadership becomes increasingly exclusive, it becomes easier to control the curiosity of the followers by presenting them with the now standard interpretation of God's rules. Indeed, much religious dogma inhibits, and even *prohibits*, the faithful laymen and laywomen from studying the religious texts for themselves![4]

For these reasons, the message of peace brought to us by the prophets is destroyed, and it becomes possible for religious leaders to falsely claim that they, and they alone, talk to God and perform His work on Earth.

The world's largest religions, which comprise Islam, Christianity and Judaism, all divide the world into "believers" and "non-believers." They all claim to worship the same God. However, along the way, the administration of these religions fell into the hands of the wrong people. These religious leaders claim, as they have done through the centuries, that the only way to find God is to subscribe to their particular group, and *only* that one, whether it be by attending a Jewish synagogue, a Christian church or an Islamic mosque. There is not even unity within the traditions themselves—just look at the many different forms that each takes! Christianity alone is divided into a countless number of sects. To be brutally honest, most religious leaders do not wish to see the faithful united—why would they? Conflict serves their purposes far too well. Instilling a false sense of superiority in their followers makes it all too easy to lead them by the nose. But nowhere in the Koran, nor in the great books of earlier prophets, has godliness been described in any manner other than the injunction: "believe in one God and be good."

Now, I am not suggesting that the various groups do not contain many good people within their numbers—of course they do. You may go into any synagogue, church or mosque and find sincere worshippers who do their best to live well. But still, the leaders of each group claim that the members of the others will not be saved. Where would they be, if their followers felt that they could just as easily worship elsewhere—and give their alms to someone else? Throughout history, religious leaders have proven that by convincing their followers that they will be damned without their leadership, they ensure their own powers, and guarantee that their pockets will always be filled by the credulous faithful.

Troubled by the inconsistency I perceived between the message related in the great books of these three religions and the way that Moslems, Jews and Christians practice their faith today, I went to visit the pastor of a Christian church. At first, he believed that I was interested in joining his group, so he was warm and friendly. He put aside some time to talk to me, and came to visit me at my business with a gift of a leather-bound Bible, which he intended to sign. When I started quoting the Bible to him, showing him what seemed to me to be inconsistencies between it and the way Christianity is lived today, he became less friendly, and was completely without helpful answers. Nor did he have anything to say when I posed those questions that always seem to be the downfall of religious leaders. Our conversation went more or less as follows: "If I am not a member of your church and do not believe in the same things as you, can I be saved?"

"No."

"Let's suppose that a little boy is born in a remote part of Africa—the best boy that ever existed. He cleans the house, obeys his parents, and behaves perfectly. However, he's been taught by his mother and father that he should worship a tree and, being an obedient boy, he does this. Now, one day, this imaginary boy's friend falls in the river, and the boy jumps in and saves him. However, before he can climb out of the river himself, he is killed by an alligator. Now the boy is facing God. He's not even a Christian, let alone a member of your church. Is he saved?"

"No."

"But why would God allow a dutiful, pious child to burn in Hell for eternity, just because he was not a follower of your religion?"

At this point, the pastor picked up the heavy, leather-bound Bible and said: "I didn't write this book, and it says that you cannot be saved unless you believe in Jesus Christ, the son of God."

"Well, sir," I wanted to know, "imagine that you are already in the otherworld, and God asks you for advice. You are to judge the little boy and decide whether he goes to Hell or to Heaven. What would you decide?"

"I'm a compassionate man," the pastor told me, "I would let the boy go to Heaven."

"But," I interjected, "if sending the boy to Hell is not a compassionate act, but is what God would do, then you're telling me that God is not compassionate—unless, of course, one is a member of your church! Wouldn't you describe God's acts as vengeful?"

At this point, our conversation drew to a rather abrupt close. The pastor left the Bible for me, but chose not to sign it. It was clear that the corruption of God's message is not restricted to Islam. Christian religious leaders have also perverted His teachings. My attempts to open constructive dialogue with Moslem clergy were even less rewarding.

As I continued researching the belief systems of the many branches of Christianity and the two main branches of the Moslem faith, Shiite and Sunni, I realized that the message of God, as it is recorded in the Koran and in the Bible, has *almost nothing at all* to do with the beliefs of modern Christians and Moslems. However, there are few things harder—for anyone—than discarding the ideas and ideology that one has been taught in childhood. As a Moslem, I grew up in a violently anti-Jewish, anti-Christian atmosphere. From babyhood, I was taught to foster a deep prejudice against these two groups. You can imagine the conflict I felt when I married a Christian American woman. Loving her, I still wanted to change her, to make her conform to my ideal of a religious Moslem woman. When I realized that it wasn't going to be easy to make her buckle under my pressure, I increased it. I considered my wife to be my personal property, and didn't want her to "expose herself" to other men wearing make-up or attractive clothes. I felt that she was mine and that I shouldn't "allow" anyone else to look at her. I believed that I was my wife's superior and expected her to follow my orders. It wasn't until she decided she wasn't taking any more and was going to divorce me that I actually sat down and really thought about what I was doing. I was forced to ask myself if I was really trying to serve God, and who was truly responsible for the rules that I was trying to follow.

This self-questioning prompted me to read the Koran, instead of just relying on the words of religious leaders. The stark contrast between the message of the holy texts and the instructions of the religious leaders I had always respected shocked me to the core, but it also left me hungry for knowledge. Over the next seven years, I developed a systematic approach to my studies, which often encompassed many hours in a day. I wrote down all the rules, both those in the Koran and those imparted by religious leaders, and compared them. In most cases, they had nothing in common at all. I extended my studies to include the Christian Bible and the teachings of many Christian religious leaders. Again, they were incredibly different. It is my belief that we should all recognize the glaring inconsistencies between the word of God as it has been recorded by prophets throughout the millennia, and the laws of religious leaders. This book presents my findings about Islam and the horrifying disparity between God's message, as revealed in the Koran, and the dogma of religious leaders.

Chapter 3

THE LOSS OF ISLAM

What is a Moslem? Is a Moslem a person who follows the teachings of the Koran? If you ask a Moslem religious leader what a Moslem is, or how one can become a Moslem, he will tell you that the key to Islam is belief in one true God and Muhammad as His prophet. The rules recorded in the Koran are very simple, including the following:

"Come close, I will recite what your Lord has forbidden you. Do not associate anything with them and show kindness towards both your parents. Do not kill your children because of poverty …do not indulge in shocking acts which you may practice either openly or in secret. Do not kill any person whom God has forbidden except in law. He has instructed you in this so that you may use your reason. Do not approach an orphan's estate before he comes of age except to improve it. Grant full measure and weight in all fairness. We do not assign any person to do more than he can cope with. Whenever you speak, be just, even though it concerns a close relative. Fulfill God's agreement. Thus has He instructed you so that you may bear it in mind. This is my rule, so follow it and do not follow paths which deviate from His."[1]

But religious leaders insist upon observance of the thousands of Moslem rules of behavior. Are these rules recorded in the Koran? In fact, they have been "revealed" over the years by a series of religious leaders who are purported to have worked day and night to extract their secrets in order to tell the humble faithful what they should and should not do. And sometimes their conclusions really stretch the imagination. For example, in the Koran, as in the Bible, it states that one should not commit adultery. That seems straightforward enough—but Shiite Moslem religious leaders have managed to invent many different rules concerning adultery, such as the one that says that if one marries one's cousin and subsequently commits adultery with her mother (who is the adulterer's aunt), the marriage to the cousin remains intact.[2]

The problem that faces Moslems today is the fact that their religious leaders have taught them a creed that has nothing to do with the Koran. They have done this by telling their followers that Islam is a very complex religion, with laws that are so hard to understand that they must be extracted by scholars and taught to the masses in a simplified form. Laws, once extracted, are written in a separate book known as the *resalah*.

So, we are told that Islam is a complex religion. It is strange then, that the Koran states *exactly the opposite*. The Koran says that the message of the prophets of God was:

"Do not worship idols. Worship the One who created you, the almighty God."[3]

Everyone who worshipped God and did not worship idols is referred to in the Koran as "Moslem." *Everyone*. The Koran names Moses, Abraham, Jesus Christ and Muhammad as exemplary Moslems:

"Were you there when death came to Jacob? Jacob told his sons, worship the God of your fathers, the God of Abraham, Isaiah and Ishmael. He is the only God, and you must die as a Moslem."[4]

In fact, in Arabic, the word "Moslem" simply means "those who have submitted themselves to God" and therefore includes both the Jews and the Christians. In the Koran, God refers to Jesus' twelve apostles as Moslems:

"But when Jesus perceived unbelief on their part, he said: Who will be my helpers in God's way? The disciples said: We are helpers of God: We believe in God and bear witness that we are Moslems."

"And when I [God] revealed to the disciples, saying: Believe in Me and My messenger, they said: We believe and bear witness that we are Moslems."[5]

As one can plainly see, Islam is not complex at all. It's very simple. Its message is that those who believe in God and do good will go to Heaven, and this basic teaching is repeated over and over again throughout the text of the Koran.

Now, Moslem religious leaders didn't like the idea of friendship and unity between all the faithful any more than did the religious leaders of the Jews when Christ's teachings challenged tribal prejudices. They were unimpressed by the notion that all Jews, Christians and Moslems worshipped the same God, and that all could be considered saved if they were good. They wanted to wield power over their own religion and profit from the fear of the people. So they began to disseminate hate, and cry that God needed a few good men, willing to give up everything for Him. For example, Ayatollah Khomeni has said that if a *jihad* (holy war) is called, even underage boys do not need to seek a parent's permission to join it.[6] The call of the religious leaders was heeded by many young men, who were willing to believe that God wanted them to fight His enemies—who, of course, were named by the same religious leaders. We must never underestimate religious leaders' potential for spreading hatred and war. The power they wield is immense, because only they are capable of convincing ordinary people that the evil deeds they commit are for the glory of God. This task is especially easy when ordinary people are uneducated. When they are educated, however, it's extremely difficult. Perhaps this is one of the reasons why Moslem religious leaders have never promoted education as they should.

Can we really consider a creed that teaches hatred to be the word of God? No true religion teaches its faithful to do anything other than offer unconditional love to friends and enemies alike.[7] Yet religious leaders are still happy to ignore the sacred texts they claim to value, and instead, revere the teachings passed to them by the heads of their organization.

"But not all religious leaders preach hatred," you may protest. It's true. For example, as a Moslem, I have to acknowledge that the Pope of the Roman Catholic church seems to be a humble and compassionate man. But even those religious leaders who preach brotherhood rarely rely upon the teachings of the great books of religion, depending instead upon the many rules created by the religious leaders who have gone before. In the case of the Catholic church, these rules have given rise to many abuses through the centuries. The current Pope is surely a good man—but the same is not true of all of his predecessors.

One example of how Catholic teaching is at odds with the teachings in the Bible lies in the doctrine of priestly celibacy. In the Bible it clearly states that a man should marry a woman, by saying:

"This is a faithful saying: if a man desires the position of a bishop, he desires a good work. A bishop must then be blameless, the husband of one wife, temperate, sober-minded, of good behavior, hospitable, able to teach, not given to wine, not violent, not greedy for money, but gentle, not quarrelsome, not covetous.

One who rules his own house well, having his children in submission with all reverence. For if a man does not know how to
rule his own house, how will he take care of the church of God?
Likewise deacons must be …the husbands of one wife, ruling
their children and their own houses well."[8]

Celibacy, a practice which was introduced centuries after the death of
Christ, is in complete opposition to the word of God as it has been reported in the Bible. But whom does the Pope choose to obey? His God, or the
teachings of the religious leaders who have gone before him? The latter, of
course!

In Islam, the consequences of the departure of religious practice from
the teachings in the holy Koran have been far-reaching. One of the reasons for this is the fact that Islam is manifested in a number of sects, each
of which despises the others. The principal two divisions of Islam are represented by the Shiite and the Sunni groups. Three of the people whom
the Sunni Moslems respect the most are cursed often by the Shiite
Moslems during their prayer ceremony: "The Curse of God on
Abobakar, the Curse of God on Omar, the Curse of God on Osman."

Moslem religious leaders and, by extension, their followers, are thus
formed in an atmosphere of hatred. Bear in mind that, in some Islamic
countries, there is no effective division between religion and state, and
you can imagine the potential for evil that this situation creates. When,
during the Iranian revolution, the religious leaders under Ayatollah
Khomeni seized power of the nation, many vivid speeches were given to
rally the masses. Whenever the excitement got the better of anyone in the
crowd, he would shout, "Takbir," thus calling the people to prayer. Their
praise of God took this form:

God is the Greatest!
God is the Greatest!
God is the Greatest!
Death to America!
Death to Russia!
Death to Israel!

Death to those who oppose Velayate Fagheh [the supreme
authority of Khomeni]!

And these people believed themselves to be godly! To use a familiar
paradigm to describe their actions: they were doing the devil's work. In
the Christian Bible, the question of those who do evil deeds in the name

of God is answered in the words of Jesus Christ when he says: "...[they ruin the work of all prophets and for that] the blood of all prophets will be required of them ... for by changing their work you are the one who actually kills them."[9]

As long as religious leaders learn their trade from each other, and do not look to the original texts of the world's great religions for inspiration, humanity will be doomed to commit evil acts in the name of God.

Moslem religious leaders—both Sunni and Shiite—seek to portray Islam as the most advanced religion of all, especially in contrast to Judaism and Christianity. They also claim that the Koran is too sophisticated for the average person to understand, and that only they, after years of study, can reveal its hidden messages. This is the greatest lie that has ever been uttered. The Koran itself states why God sent it, saying that it was given to the Arab people in particular so that they could never claim that God did not send them a prophet to speak to them in their own language and tell them to worship the one God and not idols.

"This is a blessed book We have sent, so follow it and do your duty so that you may receive mercy. So that you will not say, 'The book was sent down only to two factions before us and we have been unaware of what they study,' or: 'If the book had been sent down to us, we would be better guided than they are.' Evidence has now come to you from your Lord, as well as guidance and mercy. Who is more in the wrong than someone who rejects God's verses and even evades them?"[10]

The Koran makes it clear that it was sent to confirm the books that had already been revealed—the Torah and the Bible.

"He [God] has sent down the book to you with truth to confirm whatever existed before it. He sent down the Torah and the New Testament."

"They said: O our people! We have listened to a book revealed after Moses verifying what is before it, guiding to the truth and to the right path."[11]

The Koran also says that it contains nothing about guidance which was not already revealed in the books that came before it.

"Anything that has been told you is merely what was told messengers before you..."[12]

Furthermore, the Koran was sent so that those parts of the messages that were concealed from the people by the religious leaders of Judaism and Christianity could at last be made known to the world again.

"O followers of the book [Bible and Torah]! Indeed Our messenger has come to you making clear to you much of what you concealed of the book and to forgive a great many; indeed, there has come to you light and a clear book from God."[13]

"O followers of the book [Bible and Torah]! Indeed Our messenger has come to you explaining to you after a certain period of time from messengers before, lest you say: There came not to us a giver of good news or a warner, so indeed there has come to you a giver of good news and a warner; and God has power over all things."[14]

Moslem religious leaders try to isolate Muhammad from all other prophets by saying, "God kept the best for last." Again, this directly contradicts the Koran's teachings. The Koran says that some prophets have been given more than others—that some even talk to God. The example it gives is that of Jesus Christ, not Muhammad:

"We have preferred some of these messengers over others. Some of them were spoken to by God while others He raised in rank. We gave Jesus, the son of Mary, explanations and endorsed him by means of the Holy Spirit."[15]

Also:

"So the angels said: "Mary, God has selected you and purified you. He has selected you over all the women in the Universe. Mary, devote yourself to your Lord. Fall down on your knees and bow alongside those who so bow down… Mary, God announces word to you about someone whose name will be Christ Jesus, the son of Mary, who is well regarded in this world, and the hereafter, and one of those drawn near to God. He will speak to people while still an infant, and as an adult, and will be an honorable person."[16]

These passages clearly show that God considered Jesus to be His best prophet, not Muhammad. After all, Jesus revealed himself to be a prophet from childhood, while Muhammad was not inspired until he was forty years old. The Koran relates a number of miracles from Jesus' childhood, but says nothing of this phase of Muhammad's life. The name "Christ" is also used. Unlike Jesus, Muhammad was not a special messenger of God, but a mere helper, who brought justice to the world, and glorified the name of Jesus by setting the record straight about his deeds on earth. His mission was also to eliminate the corruption of the message of those prophets who had gone before him. On the other hand, of Jesus it is said that he was created in a similar way to Adam:

> "The creation of Jesus with God was the same as that of Adam. He created him from dust, and told him to be. And he was."[17]

Bear in mind that when God announced His creation of Adam to the angels He commanded them to bow to him.

In the contemporary world, a Moslem is a person who strives to follow the rules of the *resalah*. A true Moslem, however, is the man or woman who tries to follow the simple teachings of the Koran, and who recognizes the Jews and the Christians as his or her brothers and sisters in faith.

Chapter 4

THE RESALAH

Every religious structure is held in place by a hierarchy—a system of training and bureaucracy for religious leaders and administrations—from the local to the global, and Islam is no exception. The *ahadith*[1], or traditional rules of Islam, are disseminated by religious leaders at every level and are especially important among Shiite Moslems, resulting in a high degree of ethno-religious homogeneity.

Most Shiite Moslems seeking an advanced religious education go to the city of Ghom (an ancient city said to have been founded many years ago) in Iran, where they devote themselves to Islamic studies. At this stage they are known as *tollab*. After some years, they are referred to as *Hojat-ol-Islam*, meaning "the reasons for Islam." In order to reach the highest possible rank of ayatollah, much more study is required. If they manage to reach this point, they can write a rule book which is known as *resalah*, also referred to as Tozehol Masa-El, meaning "the explanations of the problems." These *resalahs* are manuals for living for ordinary Moslem men and women. In other words, when Moslems face a dilemma, they should refer to the *resalah* to see what God wants them to do. For example, if someone wants to know how to pray properly, they will consult the section called "prayer." Many ayatollahs have written *resalahs*, and Moslems have to decide which ayatollah to follow. Once they have made their choice, they must follow his dictates always, and cannot pick and choose between the rules of one leader and the next. Although there are minor differences from one *resalah* to the next, all are consistent about the central issues of tradition.

Mosques at local level are overseen by clergymen, or mullahs, who are equivalent to pastors or rabbis. They lead prayers and are supposed to be qualified to consult on religious matters. Like priests, they wear special clothes which they earn through study and which distinguish them from ordinary members of the Moslem community. A mullah who wears black is more venerable than one who wears white, as the black clothing indicates that he is a descendant of Muhammad or one of the Shiite's twelve *imams*. All depend upon the writings of the ayatollahs for their principal source of authoritative instruction. According to the Koran, one should go to the mosque for prayer when one can, but religious leaders say that one should attend the mosque on Fridays and all other possible occasions. In the mosque, religious leaders give sermons after prayer which emphasize the rules of the *resalah*. In this manner, ordinary Moslems become familiar with the rules of the *resalah*, while many never read the Koran in the original. Few people have any notion of the vast differences between the guidance of the Koran and the rules by which people live today.

Today's Shiite Moslem nations are affected by their heritage on every level. Their culture, economy, and international relations are all blighted by the tyranny of the *resalah*. For example, the *resalahs'* terribly oppressive rules regarding women result in their exclusion from higher levels of education and responsible positions in the workforce, thereby reducing the pool of talent considerably—even though it has long been proven that the first step towards educating a nation is the education of its mothers.

Chapter 5

THE AHADITH—
THE ADULTERATION OF
THE KORAN

A *hadith* is a message supposed to have been heard from the Prophet Muhammad, or his most loyal followers. According to the view of the Shiite sect, the most loyal followers are Ali and his eleven descendants, together forming the twelve *Imams* (leaders of Islam) after Muhammad. The term *hadith* does not, however, apply to the official divine teachings recorded in the Koran. Collectively, the *ahadith* form a series of traditional rules (most of which are recorded in a *resalah*) by which pious Moslems live. Those who heard the teachings of the prophet or his direct descendents during their lives are supposed to have passed them unaltered through the generations until the current day. In an attempt to prove the validity of the *ahadith*, religious leaders have spent lifetimes trying to figure out the originators of each one, and to trace it to the source, while investigating the qualities of each person who affirmed it to ascertain whether or not he was a righteous man. By so doing, any given religious leader can pick and choose what he wants, and say that it came from Muhammad—and thus from God—until their own ideas seem to have been divinely inspired. Although the *ahadith* are said by religious leaders to be of paramount importance, even Ali, one of the greatest followers of Muhammad, has been quoted as saying that no matter what *hadith* came from him or his children, it should not be followed unless it is completely compatible with the teachings of the Koran. Muhammad himself confirms this when he says in the Koran that he himself was not special, but merely a servant of God:

"Muhammad, you are only a messenger, and truly there were messengers before you…"

"Say: I am not the first of the messengers, and I do not know what will be done with me or with you. I do not follow anything but that which is revealed to me, and I am nothing but a plain warner."

"Say: I am only a human like you; it is revealed to me that your God is one God, therefore follow the right way to Him and ask His forgiveness; and woe to the polytheists."

"…there is nothing required of you (Muhammad) other than a plain delivering of God's message."[1]

However, the many people who believe that *ahadith* should be widely used in understanding Islam quote verses of the Koran which say: "Obey God and His prophet."[2] This is the principal justification for the widespread employment of *ahadith* in Islam, and the root of many of the problems in contemporary Moslem culture. Changing the word of the Koran would never have been possible without the use of the *ahadith*. It is this that eases Moslem minds when religious leaders tell them to do something that is not in the holy book or that is in direct contradiction to it. The religious hierarchy of Islam cannot willfully alter the text of the Koran—but it can formulate its own ideas in the form of *ahadith*, and ascribe them to historic figures of importance in the history of the faith. While the Bible has been altered throughout history, resulting in a situation whereby Christians and Jews cannot always be sure that they are following God's original message, the Koran has remained unchanged since it was revealed to Muhammad. Sadly, it does not form the basis of most contemporary Islamic practice. The justification for this lies with the fact that religious leaders tell us that whatever words the prophet or his descendents spoke are as important as the teachings of the Koran. Of course, the fact that their utterances are not necessarily reported accurately does not seem to dissuade them from this point of view. To know how to obey God and follow His teachings we simply need to read the Koran. The Koran states that when Jesus was sent to the Jews he told them:

" …fear God and obey …for this is the right way."[3]

Other prophets sent by God are quoted in the Koran as saying:

"Will you obey God and obey me?"[4]

Nowhere in the Koran does it say that a prophet's words, whether they were recorded in the Koran or not, are also the word of God. This point is especially valid, since most of the "prophets' sayings" that religious leaders have taught as *ahadith* are not recorded in the Koran. The Koran also specifically tells Muhammad to teach what is in the Koran and nothing else[5] (this is discussed in greater detail in section 9.2, later). It also tells us that all other prophets were sent only to bring the book of God to their people.[6]

In the Koran we learn that Noah told his people to fear God and obey Him[7] and also that he (Noah) wanted nothing from the people other than that they listen to him about God.[8]

When the prophet Hud came to spread the word, he said that he was a trustworthy messenger, and like Noah, said that his message was that the people should listen to him and obey God.[9] He also added that he wanted no more than for the people to listen and obey.[10]

When Thamud came, his message was exactly the same as that of his predecessors, and he added that the people should not obey the laws of "extravagant" people.[11] The prophet Lot also confirmed the message of those who had gone before.[12]

But asking the people to obey the prophets does not imply that they should copy them in everything they did or quote as doctrine a thousand years later everything that was said in a secular context. This would be a ridiculous conclusion to draw from a simple command. But since this conclusion has been engraved in the hearts of Moslems by religious leaders, to question it is to make yourself vulnerable to criticism, and even the risk of being ostracized. But I choose to question, as the Koran has said:

> "Whenever you read the Koran, we place a hidden curtain between you and those who do not believe in the hereafter. We place wrappers over their hearts, lest they comprehend it, and dullness in their ears. When you mention your Lord alone in the Koran, they even turn their backs in disgust. We are quite aware as to what they are listening [to] for when they listen to you and whenever they conspire together then wrongdoers will say, 'You are only following a man who is bewitched. Watch what sort of stories they make up about you. They have strayed away and are unable to find a way back.'"[13]

In my studies of the Koran, I have found over eighty instances where it says that those who do not follow the verse of God (the Bible, the Torah and the Koran) will be punished. Nowhere does it say that the faithful should emulate every detail of Muhammad's secular behavior on Earth. The Koran even goes so far as to say that Muhammad used it to tell people the message of God:

"This is a clear book that is revealed to you which shows the path of God."[14]

God has also said:

"Muhammad, you are only a messenger, and truly there were messengers before you..."[15]

Throughout history, religious leaders have manipulated Islamic teachings to represent their own points of view by employing the *ahadith*. In their hands, this system has been the perfect tool for altering the Koran. Today, I estimate that at least ninety percent if not all of the Shiite Moslem customs—praying, washing, eating, etc.— are in opposition to the teachings of the Koran. Yet no one questions this, as they trust that the religious leaders are fulfilling their duties as God intended. Religious leaders themselves build upon the teachings of those that preceded them, and thus the chain of ignorance grows, as without exception, they reach for the *ahadith*, and not the Koran. The religious leaders want to secure their own positions and by doing this they must not contradict their predecessors. Therefore, they must accept the *ahadith* that have already been written. This leads to the choice of man's law over God's law—a situation which was foreseen by Christ:

"For laying aside the commandment of God, you hold the tradition of men—the washing of pitchers and cups, and many other such things you do. He said to them, "All too well you reject the commandment of God, that you may keep your tradition."[16]

The Islam of today mirrors Judaism as it was at the time of Christ, with harsh laws created by men assuming dominance over the laws of God and making faith so venomous that we are forced to envision an ugly, cruel God instead of a loving one. Modern Islam has been forged from the laws that have been passed from generation to generation—nonsensical laws which were never mentioned in the Koran. The justification of the religious leaders is that Muhammad saved us by mentioning what God forgot. Yet how could there be more to the Koran when God says:

"...in this book is everything you need to know in order to find your way to Heaven."[17]

Was God lying? Were the religious leaders so smart that they knew His intention better than He? Was Muhammad greater than God, and able to add his own views to the practice of Islam? The Koran itself says that Muhammad was an uneducated man who never studied, and that he was chosen for this very reason, so that critics could not accuse him of having learnt that which was revealed to him another way:

"We repeated the verses to you so that they wouldn't say that you had studied, so that We could say these things to people who want to learn."[18]

And:

"Those who follow this prophet, who is uneducated, will find him in these books, the Bible and the Torah. He commands them to be decent and forbids them dishonor. He permits them wholesome things and forbids them unwholesome things, and relieves them of their obligation and the shackles that have lain upon them. Those who believe in him revere him and support him and follow the light which [was] sent down with him. They will be successful."[19]

To free Islam from the harsh laws of religious leaders, and bring its true, beautiful essence back, we must brush aside the web of lies that has been woven by duplicitous religious leaders. In order to do this, we must refer only to the Koran or the other holy books inspired by God, and take their words to be Gospel, as God instructed us. We must have no prejudice in our minds, free our souls from all we thought we knew, and simply take these words for what they are. If we do so, we will become great Jews, great Christians, and great Moslems. We will become one as believers in God and as people who strive to do good. When we face God, He will not ask us: "Were you a Jew, a Christian, or a Moslem?" but will simply say: "Were you good?" As Jesus and Muhammad revealed, we will be judged by our actions, by our fidelity to the guidance provided for us in the Torah, the Bible and the Koran.[20] The Koran states that in the other world, everyone will be judged according to their book. The Jews will be lined up, and Moses will be ahead of them with the Torah. The Christians will be lined up, and Jesus will be before them with the Bible. Finally, Muhammad will be before the Moslems with the Koran. God will judge each and every one according to their book and nothing but their book.[21] He will not care about *ahadith*, or ask any of us about any deeds other than our own. He will not ask which religious leaders we followed. We will simply be judged by the way we lived. In the Koran, God sends a message to the Christians and the Jews, saying,

"Tell the Christians they are of nothing unless they uphold
the Bible and tell the Jews they are of nothing unless they uphold
the Torah."
It continues,
   "… and you Moslems are of nothing unless you uphold the
Koran."[22]
Can it be that God has forgotten to mention the *ahadith*, which are a
very important part of the religious leaders' teachings? Is it possible that
He mistakenly told Muhammad that he should teach nothing but the
words of the Koran?[23] Was God mistaken in confirming that the Koran is
all anyone needs for guidance?[24] Moslems everywhere must choose
whether they want to follow the teachings of self-appointed religious
leaders, or those of God, as revealed in the Koran. It's not easy—choosing to follow the rules of God rather than the rules of man puts one at risk
of losing the trust of family and society. Most opt to accept everything
they have been taught by religious leaders and parents since childhood.
The approval they gain from those around them has short-term benefits,
but it is the weakness of such decisions that fuels the conflict between
nations and creeds.

   Let's take a look at some of the harm done by living according to the
ahadith instead of according to the laws revealed in the Koran, and the
application of common sense.

   In Ghom, a holy city about fifty miles from the capital city of Iran,
religious leaders reside and are trained. Throughout the centuries, and
until the present day, the dogma of this institution has caused untold
damage to the development of the Iranian nation. During the early twen-
tieth century, an attempt was made to provide elementary education to
girls for the first time. The woman who opened the school faced open
hostility from the religious authorities—a few days after her school was
opened, the clergy entered and attacked her, beating her severely with
wooden clubs, and also breaking all the chairs and tables. She was in the
hospital for six months, all because of a *hadith* that maintained that
women were little more than animals. Eventually, the religious leaders
conceded that primary education could be made available to girls.

   At around the same time, the first western-style pharmacy was
opened in Iran by a foreigner, who wanted to help improve the appalling
state of medicine in the country. The religious leaders informed the public that the medicines might contain some kind of alcohol, making them

too impure to eat, touch or even have in the house, and prohibited their followers from using them. They suggested as an alternative remedy for sickness the use of prayer or money given in alms to the religious authorities who would then pray for their recovery. When these methods did not prove sufficient, the religious leaders had a further resort. Saying that they were holy men, and that everything that issued from them was also holy, they offered their saliva as a cure, spitting it into cups for distribution among the people. Apparently the saliva of some religious leaders was more efficacious than that of others, and select cups of saliva became a valuable commodity. In any case, after the pharmacy had been open for some time, one of the religious leaders became ill, and no amount of prayer helped him. Finally, he went to the pharmacy, bought some medicine and used it to become well. However, while he was in the pharmacy he noticed some medicines whose names incorporated the word "acid." Several of the medications on sale contained acid of one kind or another. Now, according to dogma, any Iranians who can trace their genealogy back to one of the twelve *imams* of the Shiite are more holy than ordinary people. The term used to describe them is "asayed" which sounds rather like "acid." Because of the accidental similarity between the words, this leader returned to the mosque and gave a speech to the uneducated congregation (at this time few Iranians had received any education at all). He said that a foreigner had come to their country to sell impure substances and, what is more, to ridicule the *imams* of Muhammad by calling these substances after them.

He said, "How can we allow such a practice to take place in our own country, close to our mosques?" and he asked the people, "Who will make God happy by shutting this place down?"

The congregation marched to the pharmacy, broke everything that they found and beat the man to within an inch of his life. Escaping death, the pharmacist left Iran. Many years passed before the ban on western medicine was lifted.

There is a *resalah* that says that after people have engaged in sexual intercourse they must clean themselves from the top of their heads to the bottom of their feet. (This rule is not in the Koran.) Some years ago, the religious leaders of Ghom stated that in order to be cleansed after sex one must enter a tub, immersing the body completely three times. Soon after, showers were introduced in Iran, making the use of public baths unnecessary. Religious leaders banned the use of showers because the body was not immersed completely.

But what was really going on? In fact, the wealthy owners of public baths were paying hefty taxes to religious leaders, and they knew that if showers became popular they'd lose business, so they began exerting pressure on religious leaders, leading to the ban. Eventually, many leaders gave in, but some insisted upon the prohibition until the day they died.

The majority of Moslems in the world—even today—use their bare hands to clean themselves with water after defecating. Soap is not usually used, and hands are traditionally considered to be clean after having been dipped in water three times. Needless to say, this custom has caused many diseases—I've often wondered if it contributed to the disease that my grandmother died of at the age of fifty-four. Such is the strength of the typical Moslem's belief in religion over reason, that many modern, educated Moslems still believe that this is an appropriate way in which to clean oneself. One Moslem medical technician insisted to me that it is better for the hands to come in direct contact with human waste, and then be cleaned, than to protect them with a piece of toilet-paper, and then wash them. It's not hard to see how religious ignorance clouds the mind! Sadly, a majority of religious leaders still maintains that their way is the best for cleaning oneself after using the bathroom and the practice continues; with the result that bathrooms in Moslem countries are among the most unsanitary in the world. Ritual purity—according to the laws of the ahadith—always wins over hygiene.

The above examples of the lunacy of following man-made laws governing every aspect of life are just a few of thousands of instances. It's time we cast aside the nonsensical teachings of religious rulers and returned to the source-book of Islam—the Koran—and to the other major texts of that great triad of world religions; the Torah and the Bible.

Chapter 6

WOMEN AND ISLAM

The oppression of women is and has been widespread and vindicated by countless religions, among which we must include Islam as it has been preached and interpreted by religious leaders throughout the generations. One might assume that God is a woman-hating deity, to judge by many of the teachings of Islamic leaders. It is believed that pre-Islam Arabs commonly practiced infanticide by burying their female infants alive and contemporary Moslem teaching retains a degree of this savagery.

The Prophet Muhammad was an early pioneer in the struggle for women's rights. His was the first truly liberal voice in all of the Indo-European cultures, preaching the equality of the sexes at a time when this was literally unthinkable. How dismayed he would be to learn that the followers of Islam who claim to esteem him above all other prophets, are now members of one of the most oppressive religions of all.

Many Moslem religious leaders appear to have made it their ambition to interpret the Koran to justify the demeaning of women as much as possible. But their arguments are all without foundation. They take phrases, and even partial phrases, out of context, give them their own gloss, and pass them off as the complete word of God. For example, in Nesah, the chapter of the Koran that talks about women and gender relations, there is a verse that religious leaders have interpreted as meaning that men are better than women and that they may freely beat their wives:

"Men are supposed to take care of women for what they have been given more by God [natural differences, such as greater physical strength] and they should give their wealth to them [women]. Good women will keep themselves from other men when their husbands are away. If a man worries about his wife's infidelity, he should take her aside, talk to her kindly, [and tell her not to be unfaithful]. If she pays no heed, he should sleep apart from her, [and try to convince her still further to stop betraying him. If still she is unfaithful], only then is he entitled to hit her."[1]

The verse goes on to say that if a husband and wife are having marital problems, each should bring a person from their family to help them work out their differences.[2] Now, let's put these lines into the context of their time. Remember that they were written when most men would feel justified in murdering their wives if they suspected that they were being unfaithful, with no fear of having to face retribution. Consider the teaching in its socio-historical context. At a time when the norm was to kill first and ask questions later, the idea that one should resort to hitting only after all other means have been exhausted was truly revolutionary. Muhammad introduced the novel idea that women were entitled to be considered as full human beings, and mediated with. He never suggested that violence should be used against even the most faithless of wives, and always stressed that conflict should be solved by discussion. Marital obedience, he taught, was something that men owed to their wives, as well as women to their husbands. The Koran—the word of God as revealed by His prophet Muhammad—also provides for circumstances in which a woman fears that her husband disobeys her,[3] "obey" being a term applied equally to both men and women. Wives and husbands should obey each other; one is not subject to the other. Neither men nor women should take the law into their own hands. How much these teachings differ from the way many Moslems live today!

In an ideal world, Muhammad's radical new philosophy would have signaled the beginning of a new equality. Instead, in many Moslem cultures, women are more oppressed than ever before. Religious leaders propagate a culture that permits violence towards women by preaching female inferiority.

Most free thinkers wonder why the Koran preaches prejudice against women. In fact, many verses in the Koran can easily be interpreted by male religious leaders to the benefit of man. As in the case of anti-Jewish and anti-Christian sentiments, partial teachings are taken out of context, and are twisted and distorted until they can be interpreted as meaning the complete opposite of what was intended.

Not many Moslems understand the full ramifications of the inheritance laws in the Koran, where it states that women should inherit half as much as male heirs.[4] Taken at face value, this seems to vindicate the view commonly held by religious leaders that women are less worthy than men. But let's take a look at how the rule works within the context of family law as taught by the Koran. The Koran clearly explains that men should provide women with dowries,[5] and also with food and clothing.[6] Children must also be provided for by their fathers.[7] Now, as each generation passes its accumulated wealth on to the next, it should be distributed according to the expenses of each heir. While a woman's wealth belongs to her alone, a man is obliged to use his to support his wife and family. Therefore, while sons are supposed to inherit twice as much as daughters, the drains on their resources are much greater. If these inheritance laws are followed consistently, over time women accumulate a greater portion.

Women are not accorded an equal position within the legal system of most Moslem countries and again the justification offered is that this is what the Koran has preordained. Let's take a look at the reality of the situation. In the Koran, it says that witnesses are necessary in legal cases that arise during a business dealing, when one of the agents is not able to write or is mentally incapable and in the care of a guardian, who is responsible. Two men should be called upon to act as witnesses to the transaction. When two men cannot be found, then one man and two women should be appointed so that if one woman forgets her responsibility the other can remind her. The reasoning behind this law is not a belief in the inferiority of women, but as follows: While it is relatively easy for a man to leave his duties to attend to his legal obligations, women often have family members whom it is impossible to leave (and this must have been much more frequently the case 1400 years ago). For this reason, two women are appointed to ensure that at least one will remember the situation down the line and at least one could testify. However, it states that two witnesses are needed to testify to legally binding agreements, such as the writing of a will or in the case of divorces.[8] In these situations, the Koran never states that the witnesses must be men. Furthermore, the Koran states that if a man reports that a woman has committed adultery, he should receive seventy lashes—unless he can provide four objective witnesses of either sex to prove the crime![9]

Perhaps the most visible symbol of women's oppression under Islam is the use of head coverings, common to most Moslem cultures. Many Moslems, religious leaders and women alike, insist blindly that the Koran teaches that women should be covered. In fact, not one single reference discusses hair-coverings for women! Instead, the holy book touches on the subject of appropriate dress and modesty for both men and women, saying that they should "cover their eyes from lusting" and keep their private parts covered from the gaze of others (women's breasts are also considered to be private).[10] Hair coverings are never mentioned.

One chapter of the Koran, known as *Ahzab*, is often the subject of controversial discussion, being frequently cited by religious leaders as proof of God's plans for female modesty. In this chapter, God reveals His intentions for the wives of the prophet Muhammad, saying:

"Tell your wives that they are not the same as other women. When men want to speak with them, they [the wives] should be behind a covering."[11]

Muhammad's wives were also instructed not to marry after the prophet's death. Now, it is clear elsewhere that divorced or widowed women should marry again—these teachings refer to *Muhammad's wives only*, because as the prophet's cohorts and early ambassadors uniting the previously fragmented Arab peoples, they had to be above reproach. This extract from the Koran is the one that has most frequently been quoted to justify the oppression of women. In fact, these teachings refer to specific people, at a specific time, and in specific circumstances. Furthermore, the Koran states that if Muhammad's wives felt unable to abide by these rules, they should be given their dowries and allowed to leave.

In the Koran it states that the wives and daughters of Muhammad and other women of faith should cover themselves, so that they could be seen to be modest, and left unmolested by men.[12] Moslem religious leaders, disregarding the Koran's teaching which stresses that the genitals and breasts should be covered, preach that women should be entirely hidden by their clothes. Modern Moslems should remember that this was a teaching given to women living at a particular point in history. For modern women to avoid harassment, they should dress according to contemporary standards of decency. Furthermore, any harassment towards a woman, regardless of her standards of modesty, should be understood to be the fault of the harasser, not the victim. Although it is the responsibility of governments to provide laws ensuring women's security, during Muhammad's time there were no such protective laws.

Less apparent to those living outside Islam is the regular oppression of women in the context of worship. In the mosque, women are expected to pray in a separate section of the building, located behind the men. Most mosques also have separate doors—one for men and one for women, and the women's door is usually the back door. The Koran says nothing to suggest that this is the correct way to conduct public worship. Instead, the book constantly stresses that one should respect one's mother above all others. How can this teaching be reconciled with the idea of forcing women to pray behind men? This tradition has led to the common practice of Moslem women walking behind men, as if they were inferior beings. Many Moslems are deeply shocked when they come to countries like America and see that in other civilizations women can walk in front of men, and enter doors first. Adjusting to this very visible symbol of equality is painfully difficult for many religiously observant Moslems, and will remain so for as long as the religious leaders of Islam hold sway.

As well as justifying the regular oppression of Moslem women, religious leaders teach that women should be ashamed of a biological function created by God—menstruation. While all healthy women of childbearing age menstruate, and should see this as a blessing and a sign of good health, Moslem women are taught from girlhood to consider themselves as impure during this time. They are not allowed to offer prayers to God during these days, and nor are they allowed to fast in the holy month of Ramadan, thus excluding them from one of the most important rites of the Moslem faith. Exclusion of this nature has caused certain religious leaders to claim that women's faith is "incomplete" compared to that of men. If faith were a matter of material substance, then blood, food or other substances could cause it to become impure. However, since faith is of spiritual substance, how can it be made impure by blood generated by a natural biological process? Again, the Koran has nothing at all to say about women's prayer during these days. The only thing it says is that men should not insist upon having sexual relations with their wives when they are menstruating, as this may be difficult for the women.[13]

The laws of religious leaders regarding women are sometimes so reactionary that if they were preached in any modern university, they would do more to contribute to the exodus of Moslem women from the faith than anything else. About fifteen years ago, I attended a seminar for Shiite Moslem people at one of the universities in California. Afterwards, everyone gathered around the ayatollah, a man named Ghazvinie. He had been sent to America by another supreme religious leader to spread

Islam, and to help the development of Shiite Moslem communities in the country. I was studying karate at the time, and asked him his opinion about the propriety of practicing with women (bear in mind that both men and women were well-padded in protective gear).

His answer was: "You can't practice with women. Not because it's forbidden to touch women, but because you are so superior physically, that you should be embarrassed to do so."

The next day, after attending another typical speech, many of the women present gathered around the ayatollah, while a man asked: "Can we allow our wives to wear make-up in public?"

"No," answered the ayatollah, "and if you do, you will be among the people whom God calls *dayous* in the other world." This means: "a person to whom God will never speak" (in the Koran, God says that He will only refrain from speaking to those who conceal the word of God as revealed in the book, and that these people will be punished).[14] Another man at the meeting joined in: "But sometimes my wife and I fight so much that we might end up divorcing about this subject."

Ayatollah Ghazvinie said: "Son, women and children are like a herd of sheep. You must be a good shepherd, and guide them to the right path. Don't allow the sheep to guide you."

At that point, a few of the women were so angry that they actually got up and left. I hope that their disillusionment with this religious leader prompted them to explore the realities of Islam for the first time in their lives.

As I have already mentioned, the Prophet Muhammad was an early voice preaching against the mistreatment of women, and in favor of their equality in the eyes of society and of the law. His teachings about gender relations have been ignored—in fact, they have been systematically overturned by generations of misogynist religious leaders. Only when women and men can pray and live side by side in an environment of mutual respect, will true Islam be lived the way prophet Muhammad intended.

Chapter 7

AMERICA AND ISLAM

O ver the millennia, super-powers have come and gone, from the empires of the Arabs, the Romans and the Ethiopians, to those located in what are now Mexico and Peru. All have made contributions to the advancement of culture and civilization—and all have done so, at least in part, by subjugating weaker peoples and imposing limitations, taxes and other injustices upon them. The Romans gave us the Roman alphabet which is used by many modern languages, including English—but they also tortured and crucified those who protested against them. The Arabs and the Greeks were the inventors of modern mathematics, but they—as did the Romans—built their society upon a system of slavery and the subjugation of the weak. The Aztecs and the Inca were advanced scholars and architects, but they practiced widespread human sacrifice. The many advances of these complex societies did not come without a price, and that price was paid by the weak and the oppressed.

America may not be perfect—it is not—but with all its faults it is still the most free and just super-power that the human race has ever seen. Mistakes in domestic and foreign policy may be made, but the oppression of the weak is *never* a deliberate function of the government of the United States. Of all the constitutions in the world, that of America is the one that most approximates the laws of the New Testament and the Koran.

According to the Koran, one of the important rules is not to submit to doubt,[1] and doing so is a sin.[2] One must always know the facts before making an accusation. It is deeply shocking to note that many Moslem religious leaders blame America for all the problems suffered by the Moslem people. They accuse America of unspeakable acts. For example, the tragedy of September 11th, 2001 has been said by some to be the work of America itself. Their crazed reasoning states that all Jewish investors withdrew their money from the stock market immediately before the attack. They believe that America advised them to do so, because of its love for the Jewish people. Accusations like this are only accepted by those who are totally lacking in education and more inclined to accept idle gossip than the truth. Any reasonable person would ask that such statements be backed up with evidence. But let's see what light the teachings of the Koran can shed on the reality of the situation in America.

When God created Adam, the angels questioned Him, saying: "Why create such a thing?" God answered: "You don't know what I know about him." The angels asked: "What makes him special?" God said: "I will demonstrate."[3] In the Koran and in the Bible it says that God taught His names to the angels, and to Adam, saying: "Tell me about these words."[4] The angels merely repeated the words, but Adam answered in much more detail.

This demonstration shows the importance of the creation of humankind, in which we see a creature capable not only of honoring God, but also of understanding God's power, by discovering His creations in detail.

He who has a limited knowledge of mathematics admires the one who knows how to multiply. The power of the person who knows how to multiply can be recognized as a higher knowledge by the person who can only add. But multivariable calculus remains beyond the grasp of both those who only know how to add or how to multiply. The person who has mastered it is vastly superior in terms of mathematical knowledge. Those who lag behind know that the person who mastered it is superior, but can't imagine the extent of this superiority.

The angels know only what God has taught them, but they lack the intellect of Adam.[5] Adam—humankind, in other words—can learn, can research, can investigate all of God's creation, and can build educational institutions, which are the center of teaching and learning. By using their brains, people can begin to understand the depths of God's power in at least a few areas, something which angels are unequipped to do.[6] God is pleased to use humankind as proof of the majesty of His creation. In order to use our talents to please God, we must create a system whereby all humans strive to develop their intellects to their maximum potential. Anyone can see that this can only be accomplished by means of a very organized educational system, in which one person's findings can be taught to others throughout the generations. Little by little, learning accumulates, and perhaps eventually humankind will have learned enough to be able to understand God more clearly than any other creature. Which, of all the cultures in the world, has achieved the most in terms of learning and intellectual development? The United States! And by seeking always to improve the quality of learning and intellectual life, America has become the land that is home to God's most loyal people.

Moslem religious leaders are quoted as saying that ink in the pen of he who studies is holier than the blood of martyrs. Billions of drops of ink are used every day in the United States of America, and billions have been used every day throughout centuries of learning. This metaphor represents not millions, but billions of people applying themselves to learning and advancement. If the Moslem leaders are correct, each of these people is more sacred than a thousand martyrs—and yet most of them are not Moslem!

How can we read the Koran and consider ourselves to be Moslem and still aspire to kill the people about whom God is boasting to the angels? If God praises Christians in the Koran, then how can we fail to see their greatness? Most Moslems have been raised in an environment of prejudice against foreigners, and it takes little to fan the flames of hatred for Americans or Jews.

Not long ago, I had the following discussion with a Moslem acquaintance:

I said, "Without America, we would never have received the education we did. God has said in the Koran that we must be thankful for what He has given us, but how can we obey Him if we are not thankful to America? Russia closed its country's door to foreigners for many years but America made people welcome so that they could boost the nation's potential. The American way of life is a beautiful one, in which taxes are put to good use to make lives better. Throughout history, most tax collectors have used the money they collect for themselves. In Iran, taxes mostly went to the Shah and his family, but in America, a free education is provided for everyone. Each person is allowed to choose how he or she will live—the good can become even better, and the bad can choose to be bad. Everyone is free to follow the dictates of conscience. My American education allowed me to think for myself for the first time, and to stop following the teachings of hate-filled religious leaders. Shouldn't we thank America?"

"For what?" my companion asked, "I paid higher tuition fees to go to school than the Americans, and besides, this country is not as fair as you say. It is a bad country, and there are plenty of people who suffer here. America is not so wonderful as you think."

I said, "No one is perfect. But can we just agree that we should thank America for providing us with an environment in which we pay for and receive an excellent education?"

She replied, "I have nothing to thank America for." She was beginning to get angry. (The same woman was in the process of obtaining American citizenship, while apparently oblivious to the hypocrisy of this.)

I said, "Until we see how great the American system is, and praise American achievements, we will never learn from Americans. And since we are so far behind their system, we need to learn from them before we can achieve anything by ourselves, just as a baby has to learn how to walk before running. First of all, I have to thank America for letting me enter this country. Otherwise, I would have had to live in India or in an Arab country where I would never have enjoyed the standard of living I have today. And I also need to thank America for the education I was able to receive in its colleges. I was welcomed to this society and now I am proud to be part of it."

America represents the best of the whole world. Just about every racial and ethnic group that walks the face of the Earth is present in the United States. American Indians, African Americans, Arab Americans, Americans of European descent—all have contributed and continue to contribute to the nation's greatness. The truly revolutionary message brought to humanity by Christ and Muhammad is that we should all attempt to transcend tribalism and embrace the common good. Nowhere in the world is there a society so plural as that in the United States, nor one so devoted to the equality of human beings, regardless of origin. Is this not something to praise? One of the final hurdles that we must leap before becoming truly civilized is that of the racism and petty thinking that inhibits the development of many a potentially wealthy and egalitarian society. Sadly, such thinking typifies modern Moslem society, while the United States of America, as imperfect as it may be, represents the greatest advance towards a completely free and integrated society to date.

Chapter 8

HOLY WAR
(JIHAD)

*(Jihad in the Koran versus popular interpretations
of Jihad by those in authority)*

In today's worrying political climate, the term and concept of *"jihad"* is preoccupying many people. But few people understand the original, and true, meaning of the term which is derived from the Arabic word "jahd," meaning "endeavor" or "trying."

In the Koran there are many references to holy war.[1] Bear in mind that holy war is not intended to be merely war in the usual sense of word, but also refers to the struggle of following God's path despite all obstacles. But the Koran has never promoted the killing of innocent people. It has always said that one should only kill in self-defense—fighting only against those who evict you from your home, and try to kill you. One should only fear God, for He will help the righteous in their battles. After defeating an enemy, one must not oppress the losers, but instead treat them justly and without harshness. To demonstrate how great a sin it is to kill, God relates the following:

Adam had two sons, one named Cain and one named Abel. One killed the other because he was jealous. In the Koran, God said that it should be noted that when one killed the other, succeeding generations of humans were limited to only the offspring of the survivor. This means that he who kills must be punished by God, not only for killing one person, but for killing an entire generation.[2]

Clearly, God means us to understand that it is wrong to kill, and that the outcome of such actions is disastrous. By killing one person, one destroys the potential of generations to come, and is responsible for the loss of thousands—millions—of potential lives. In Muhammad's time, a holy war was instigated only when the enemy consistently refused to leave Muhammad and his followers alone, seeking them out and trying to kill them. After many years, Muhammad was finally granted God's permission to defend himself with force. The verses in the Koran which discuss killing other human beings refer to fighting against evil people, called "the non-believers" or "the scribers who want to kill you." For religious leaders to declare holy war against anyone or any country, *it must be as a defensive action, not an offensive one.*[3] For terrorists to think of themselves as holy warriors is like the devil himself talking about the words of God. The devil has many armies, but the most dangerous are those that he fools by convincing them that they are holy, godly men. These are his best warriors, for they do not fear death or the loss of wealth. All they seek is to make God happy, and the devil has convinced them that the only way to God is through him. In this way, the most evil act—the slaughter of innocent people—can be committed in the name of God. The best demonstration of this occurred on September 11th, 2001, when a group of misguided zealots sacrificed their own lives, and those of thousands of innocent civilians, in the name of God. Although many countries have suffered losses through aggression, this is different, because the enemy is claiming to be killing on behalf of God.[4] For this reason it is imperative that these evil men be asked to demonstrate the Koran's justification for their deeds. One must always ensure that they do not show extracts from the Koran (or the Bible or Torah) out of context.

Throughout the entire Koran, holy war is described as being a war between believers and non-believers. (America, described as "One nation under God…" can hardly be considered to be a country of non-believers.) The idea that a country should be condemned for being superior in wealth or in any other way is ridiculous.

According to Muhammad, the biggest *jihad* of all is not fought in the battlefield, with guns and tanks. The biggest *jihad* is the fight between good and bad in the hearts of individual men and women.

After one of the last wars won by Muhammad, the people asked him, "Is *jihad* over now?"

The prophet answered, "The lesser *jihad* is over, but you must prepare for the greatest battle of all, the *Jihad* of Akbar (the greatest *jihad*) The greatest battle is about to begin."

"Are we about to fight a great empire?" the people wanted to know.

Muhammad replied, "The greatest *jihad* is fought at home, when you try to live a life of godliness in every way. In everything you do, you should remember God. You should respond to sins committed against you with good deeds. If you can do all this, you have won the greatest *jihad*."

I agree with the Koran when it says that believers should engage in *jihad*—the *jihad* that is waged every day in the hearts of ordinary men and women as they struggle between the unkind thoughts that occur to us all and the true desire to be as good as they can. It is time to fight for the original meaning of the term, and struggle to fulfill God's commands to His people on Earth.

It is ironic that *jihad*, as it is described in the Koran, best describes what has occurred in America since its birth as a nation—the continuous struggle for excellence.

Chapter 9

JUDGE THE KORAN FOR YOURSELF

My purpose in writing this book is not to tell you what to think about Islam or about the Koran. Instead, my hope is that readers become enabled to judge the message of the Koran for themselves, be they Moslem, Christian, Jew or of another religious belief. In this chapter, you will get a chance to read some of the more controversial parts of the Koran and ask yourself what meaning they convey. I'm confident that you will see that the contorted interpretations ascribed to them have nothing at all to do with the original meanings of the sacred text.

When I am asked how I dare to claim to be able to understand the Koran better than a religious authority, my answer is that the sacred text itself says that it has been written so as to be easily understood.[1] Besides, how can it be claimed that the message of God is obscure to the point of being unintelligible to educated, secular people? Is God so subtle in His ways that He seems to say one thing, while implying the complete opposite? I am an engineer, not a theologian, and yet I am very willing to claim that I have understood the message of the Koran. The holy book was not written for a select group of highly trained "scholars"—it was God's gift to humanity.

In this chapter, I include quotations from the Koran on all of the most controversial topics associated with modern Islam. You yourself can judge, on reading the extracts in their proper context, whether true Islam—the Islam of the Koran—is a religion of hate or of love.

Christian readers especially will be interested to learn that the Koran teaches that Jesus was God's best prophet, and that Christians will be placed above non-believers until the Day of Judgment. Does it surprise you to learn that the Koran may have been intended for Christians, to confirm all that they had been taught by Christ?

Moslem readers must make a tangible effort to question all of the customs and beliefs that until now they have assumed to be confirmed in the Koran. Does the Koran dictate the terrible hardships that many Moslems endure in the name of religion? Does it tell women to cover themselves from head to toe in shame?

The current political climate has thrust contemporary Islam and the Koran into the spotlight. Many people, Moslem and non-Moslem alike, have picked up the Koran for the first time. Radio talk shows abound with discussions of various verses. Many non-Moslems have cited extracts from the Koran as "proof" of the inherent violence of Islam. They are as inaccurate as are the devout Moslems who quote the many man-made traditional rules handed to them by corrupt or self-serving religious leaders.

I am not going to use this chapter to give you my own interpretation of some of the more controversial extracts of the Koran. Instead, I will quote—in their entirety—the verses that have given rise to most discussion. You will be the judge. The quotations below have not been modified in any way, and I have not included the biased opinions of religious leaders from any group. However, I *do* discuss common misinterpretations of the verses, and comment on what seem to be logical conclusions, drawn from a simple reading.

9.1 Quotations about women's covering

As you know, Islamic women cover themselves from head to toe. If this practice is a law that comes from God, any non-biased reader should be able to understand it from reading the relevant sections of the Koran. Instead, none of the verses below say that women should cover their hair, suggesting instead that *both* men and women should keep their private parts covered. Moslem religious leaders insist that women must cover their whole bodies, and say that anyone who argues with them is a corrupt Westerner. They maintain that if they relax the taboo on showing any part of a woman's body, that the floodgates of corruption will be opened and Moslem culture destroyed.

However, the opposite is true. Because people are forced to behave in a manner entirely unnatural to them, Moslem societies have already become corrupt, without any influence from the West at all. Iranians, if they are being honest, will admit that the behavior of Iranian men has deteriorated since the revolution of the Ayatollah. The harassment of women has increased—even my mother, who is almost sixty years old, is afraid to walk in the streets, where she is often sexually harassed by young men. Because crimes of sexual harassment and rape go largely unpunished, this form of violence is widespread. A woman who has been raped is considered to be culpable, unmarriageable. This view, while endorsed by most Moslem religious leaders, has no correlation in the Koran.

Now, let's review the verses in the Koran that teach about the issue of women's clothing, and see what lesson any reasonable person would derive from them.

7:25 "Children of Adam, We have sent you down clothing with which to cover your private parts and to dress in. Yet the clothing of heedfulness is best!" That is one of God's signs, so that they may bear it in mind.

7:26 Children of Adam, do not let Satan tempt you just as he turned your father and mother [Adam and Eve] out of the Garden, stripping them of their clothing in order to show them their private parts. Satan and his tribe watch you from where you do not see them! We have placed devils as guardians for those who do not believe.

7:29 Children of Adam! Take your adornment at every place of worship; and eat and drink, but do not be prodigal [wasteful]; God does not like the prodigal.

7:30 Say: "Who has forbidden the ornament of God which He brought forth for His servants and the good things of His providing?" Say: "In this world, these belong to the believers and are exclusively theirs in the otherworld. We make these signs clear for a people who are able to know."

7:31 Say: "My Lord has only forbidden indecencies, the apparent ones as well as the hidden ones, and sin, and oppressive injustice, and that you make anything or anyone partner with God, and that you say God says this and that, when you are unsure."

24:30 Say to the believing men, that they cast down their eyes and guard their private parts; that is purer for them. God is aware of the things they do.

24:31 And say to the believing women, that they cast down their eyes and guard their private parts, and reveal not their adornment except that which comes before them, and they must cover their bosoms with a covering cloth, and not reveal their adornment except to their husbands, or their fathers, or their husband's fathers, or their sons, or their husband's sons, or their brothers, or their brother's sons, or their sister's sons, or their women, or what their right hands own, or such men as attend them, not having sexual desire, or children who have not yet attained knowledge of women's private parts; nor let them stamp their feet, so that their hidden ornament may be known. And turn all together to God, O you believers; in this manner will you prosper.

24:59   Those women sitting around who no longer expect to marry will meet with no objection if they take off their clothing, though without displaying their charms. Yet it is best for them to act modestly. God is Alert, Aware.

33:59   O Prophet, say to thy wives and daughters and the believing women, that they cover themselves with a covering cloth, so it is likelier they will be known as modest women, so they won't be troubled. God is all-forgiving, all compassionate.

The verses above seem very straightforward—one should not display one's private parts—which, in the case of women, include the breasts. However, religious leaders read much more into the verses than that. They say that since women are not supposed to show their charms, they should cover themselves from head to toe, as their whole bodies are so beautiful as to be considered "charms." In verse 24:31, it states that women should cover their breasts. The word used to describe the cloth they should use is khomor which, although it may be used to describe any cloth, is still used for the cloth that women use to cover their hair. In the Middle East, both men and women tend to cover their heads because of the heat—but there is nothing in the Koran that says that this should be done in all circumstances. Most religious leaders interpret verse 33:59 as saying that women should cover their entire bodies rather than just their private areas.

Now, why would God bother to specify that women should not show their private parts, if He had already told them that they should cover their entire bodies? This just doesn't make sense! Where the word "*khomor*" is used to describe the cloth used by women to cover their breasts, it is used in the sense of any cloth, which can be used to cover anything.

It is not a term that describes an all-body wrap. Readers of the Koran should not assign meanings to God's instructions that are not there. Finally, certain rules of the Koran regarding the appropriate behavior of women refer to the prophet's wives and only the prophet's wives, because of their delicate political role in the uniting of the Arab peoples. The Koran states of these women: "Muhammad, tell your wives that they are not like other women."[2] Because of this injunction, instructions given to them should not be considered to apply to all women everywhere, especially when easily understood information about appropriately modest dress has already been supplied. When the Koran was written, many people lived in relatively primitive conditions, and basic instructions about hygiene and modesty were supplied by God through His messenger, Muhammad. Sadly, these simple instructions have been contorted by religious leaders and have become weapons in the war against female liberty.

We cannot be surprised when unsophisticated, illiterate women allow themselves to be convinced by their religious leaders and husbands that they should be ashamed of their bodies, and cover themselves completely. But educated, modern, Moslem women allow themselves to be victims of the same teachings—often without ever reading the Koran for themselves!

9.2 The Koran's representation of itself

The truth about the Koran has been successfully concealed from the world by generations of religious leaders, and the tool they use to suppress the words of God are the rules and regulations known as the *ahadith*. The thousands of laws that are the *ahadith* have no correspondence with the Koran, and enable the ambitious to rule their people by subjecting them to these destructive rules. The theological justification, if it may be so called, is that the *ahadith* were laws (supposedly) uttered by Muhammad, although they are unrecorded in the Koran. Shiite Moslems extend the *ahadith* to include anything said by the prophet or one of his twelve *imams*. In practice, the *ahadith* (specifically those that completely contradict the Koran) are real tools of evil. But let's examine them rationally.

If, in the Koran, it is stated that it contains all the rules necessary for living a godly life,[3] then why are the *ahadith* necessary? Here, we'll examine what religious leaders have to say about the Koran, and what God's message in the Koran teaches us about the nature of the holy book.

Moslem religious leaders insist that:

❖   The Koran is a powerful book that should be used for guidance in conjunction with the sayings of Muhammad.

❖   Such is its complexity, that ordinary people desperately need the help of religious leaders to understand God's intentions as revealed in its verses.

❖   The Koran should only be interpreted by a highly qualified supreme religious leader.

❖   The Koran is superior to both the Bible and the Torah, and is the completion of all religious works that preceded it.

❖   Arabic is a sacred language, which is why the Koran is written in that language.

❖   The Arabic of the Koran is very hard to understand; one should be either a native speaker of Arabic or at least highly qualified in that language, in order to even understand the words written.

❖   To simply translate the Koran from Arabic to another language is extraordinarily difficult.

I counter these arguments as follows:

❖   The Koran is indeed a powerful book, and it should be used without contamination from other sources, even the supposed and actual sayings of the Prophet Muhammad.

❖   No religious leadership is necessary to interpret its teachings. The job of religious leaders should be simply to repeat exactly what is in the Koran to the people.

❖   The Koran is wonderfully simple to understand, and at no point is there any reason to doubt its message.

❖   Unlike the arts or the sciences which must be studied for many years in order to be practiced, the Koran provides us with a simple message from God for those whose hearts are pure and wish to follow God's path. No sophisticated learning or ability is necessary to understand it.

❖   The Koran is not superior to its predecessors (the Bible and the Torah) and it does not represent an improvement on what went before, but a reiteration and confirmation of the same message.

❖   God chose the Arabic language as the medium for the message so that the Arab peoples would cease worshipping idols, and so that they would be unable to claim that the message of God was never sent to them in their own language.

❖ The Arabic of the Koran is not particularly complex—it can be easily understood by Arabic speakers, and readily translated into any other language.

Now, let's take a look at the evidence item by item and compare the message of the Koran with that disseminated by the religious leaders. Religious leaders, as we've seen, say that the Koran should be used in conjunction with the *ahadith*, that it is so complex that ordinary people need help in interpreting it, and that this interpretation can only be done by highly trained experts. I believe that the Koran should be used in its unadulterated form, without input even from the Prophet Muhammad,[4] that it is simple and impossible to misunderstand, and that anyone able to read it is able to comprehend its message. But what is the evidence in the book itself? The following verses explore this:

2:1 This book which contains no doubt, is a guide to those who guard [against evil].

2:115 Those whom We[5] have brought the book, recite it in the way it should be recited; such men believe in it. Those who disbelieve in it will be the losers.

2:181 The month of Ramadan is when the Koran was sent down as guidance for mankind and with explanations for guidance, and as a standard [by which to live].

2:221 ...and makes clear His communications to man, that they may be mindful.

4:84 Have they not meditated on the reading? If it had come from some other source than God, they would have found a great deal of contradiction in it.

4:106 We have sent the book down to you with the truth so that you may judge among mankind by means of what God has shown you.

6:34 Messengers before you have been rejected, yet they held firm [despite] being rejected and abused, until Our support came to them. There is no way to change God's words! News from [other] emissaries has already come to you.

6:104 Insights have come to you from your Lord; anyone who observes

[them] does so for his own sake, while anyone who acts blindly has himself to blame. I am not [set up as] a guardian over you.

6:115   Your Lord's word has been completed so far as [its] credibility and justice are concerned; there is no way to change His words. He is the alert, the aware.

6:156   This is a blessed book We have sent down, so follow it and do your duty so that you may receive mercy.

7:1-2   A book has been sent down to you, so do not let your chest feel it is under any constraint because of it, so you may warn by means of it; a reminder for believers. Follow whatever has been sent down to you by your Lord and do not follow any sponsors besides Him; yet how seldom do you remember!

7:50   We have given them the book; We have spelled it out knowingly as a guideline and mercy for folk who believe.

7:169   As for those who hold onto the book and keep up prayer—We shall never forfeit reformers' wages.

7:202   If you had not brought them any sign, they would [still] say: "Why didn't you pick one out?" Say: "I follow only what has been inspired in me by my Lord. These are insights from your Lord, as well as guidance and mercy for folk who believe."

10:1   These are verses from the wise book.

10:64   [You] will have good news concerning worldly life as well as the hereafter. There is no way to alter God's words; that will be the supreme achievement.

10:82   God verifies the truth through His own words no matter how the guilty ones may hate it.

11:1-2   ...[This is] a book whose verses are decisive, and have been set forth in detail in the presence of someone [who is] wise, informed, that you will serve only God [alone]: "I am a warner, a herald from Him to you."

13:1   These are verses from the book; what has been sent down to you by your Lord is the truth, even though most men do not believe so.

13:29   Thus we have sent to a nation—nations have passed away long before it—so you may recite to them what we have inspired you with, even though they disbelieve in the mercy-giving! Say: "He is my God: There is no God except Him. On Him do I rely and toward Him my repentance."

14:1 We have sent down a book to you in order to bring men out of darkness into light by their Lord's permission, towards the road of the powerful, the praiseworthy.

15:1 These are verses from the book, and a clear reading.

15:9 We Ourself have sent down the reminder just as We are safeguarding it.

15:90-93 Such as We have sent down for the quibblers who have torn the Koran apart. By your Lord, We shall question them all about whatever they have been doing!

16:91 ...We have sent the book down to you to explain everything, and for guidance and mercy and as good news for Moslems.

17:9-10 The Koran guides one to something that is more straightforward and reassures believers who perform honorable actions; they shall have great earnings.

17:43 We have already spelled out matters in this reading so they will notice it, even though it only adds to their disgust.

17:84 We sent down something from the Koran [to serve] as healing and a mercy for believers, while wrongdoers are only increased in loss.

18:1-3 Praise be to God, who has sent down the book for His servants and has placed no distortion in it, [it is] straightforward, so He may warn about serious violence from himself and give good news to believers who perform honorable deeds. They will have a handsome wage, to bask in forever and ever.

18:26-27 Quote whatever has been revealed to you from your Lord's book: there is no one who may change His words, nor will you ever find any sanctuary except in Him. Restrain yourself concerning those who appeal to their Lord in the morning and evening, wanting His presence; yet do not let your eyes wander too far from them, desiring the attraction of worldly life. Do not obey anyone whose heart We allow to neglect remembering Us, so he pursues his own whim. He will become dissipated.

18:52 We have spelled out every sort of example for mankind in this

Koran, yet every man uses it just for argument in most cases.

19:97 We have made it easy for your tongue so you may announce good news about it to those who do their duty, and warn headstrong folk by means of it.

21:10 We have sent down a book to you, which contains your reminder. Will you not use your reason?

22:8 Yet some men argue about God without having any knowledge or guidance, nor any enlightening book.

24:53 … the messenger has only to announce things clearly.

25:34-35 Those who disbelieve say: "Why has not the Koran been sent down to him in one single piece?" [It has been done] like that so your vitals may be braced by it; We have phrased it deliberately. They will not come to you with any example unless We will bring you the truth and something even finer as a commentary.

26:193-196 The faithful spirit has descended with it upon your heart that you may be of the warners in plain Arabic and most surely the same is in the scripture of the ancients.

26:1 These are verses from the clear book.

27:1-2 These are verses from Koran and clear book [offered] for guidance and as good news for believers.

30:58 We had set forth every sort of example for men in this Koran. Yet even if you brought them some sign, those who disbelieve will still say: "You [all] are only trifling!"

31:5 Some men buy up sporting tales to mislead from God's way without having any knowledge, and they take it as a joke. They will have shameful torment.

31:19 Do you not see how God has harnessed whatever is in Heaven and whatever is on Earth for you? He has lavished His favor on you both publicly and privately. Yet some men will still argue about God without having any knowledge or guidance, nor any enlightening book!

33:2 Follow whatever you are inspired with by your Lord; God is informed about what you [all] are doing.

35:28 What We have revealed to you from the book is the truth confirming what has preceded it [the Torah and the Bible]. God is informed and observant concerning His servants.

36:69 We have not taught him any poetry nor would it be fitting for him. It is a merely a reminder and a clear reading.

38:28 We have sent down a book to you that is blessed, so prudent men may ponder over its verses and thereby be reminded.

39:1-5 The revelation of the book [occurs] through God, the powerful, the wise! We have sent the book down to you with the truth, so serve God sincerely: religion belongs to Him. Pure religion belongs to God [alone]! Those who take on [other] patrons instead of Him [claim]: "We do not serve them except to bring us closer to God in homage." God will judge among them about whatever they have been differing over; God does not guide anyone who is a disbelieving liar.

39:28-29 We have made every sort of comparison for mankind in this reading so that they may be reminded by an unambiguous Arabic Koran so that they may do their duty.

39:42 We have sent you down the book with truth for mankind. ...

40:37 The ones who argue about God's signs without any authority to do so... incur the greatest disgust so far as God is concerned and so far as those who believe are concerned. Thus God seals off every overbearing oppressor's heart.

40:58 Those who argue about God's signs without having any authority to do so only feel pride within their breasts; they shall never achieve anything. Take refuge with God; He is the alert, the observant.

40:71 Have you not considered how the ones who argue about God's signs actually disregard them?

41:40 The ones who distort Our signs are never hidden from Us. Is someone who will be cast into the fire better, or someone who will come safely through on Resurrection Day? Do whatever you may wish: He is observant of anything you do.

41:42 No falsehood shall approach it from either in front of it or behind it, since it is a revelation from someone wise and praiseworthy.

44:3 In it [the Koran] every wise matter is set forth.

44:58   We have made it easy for your tongue [to recite] in order that they may bear this in mind.

45:5-10 Those are God's signs, which We recite to you for the truth, so in what report will you believe if not in God and His signs? How awful will it be for every shameful sinner who hears God's signs recited to him, then proudly persists as if he had never heard them. Announce some painful torment to him! Whenever he learns anything about Our signs, he takes them as a joke. Those shall have shameful torment: Beyond them there lies Hell. Anything they have earned will not help them at all, nor will anything they have adopted as patrons instead of God. They will have awful torment! This means guidance, while those who disbelieve in your Lord's signs will have painful punishment as blight.

45:19   These are insights for mankind, as well as guidance and mercy for folk who are convinced.

45:24   Whenever Our clear verses are recited to them, their argument is merely to say: "Bring back our forefathers if you are so truthful."

46:6   When Our clear signs are being recited to them, those who disbelieve will remark about the truth once it comes to them: "This is sheer magic!"

47:26-27 Will they not meditate on the Koran, or do they have locks on their hearts? Satan has seduced the ones who turned their backs after guidance had been explained to them, and he is dictating to them.

50:45   Remind anyone who fears My warning by means of the Koran.

54:17, 22, 32, 40 We have made the Koran easy for guidance, will anyone be guided? [Repeated four times.]

81:27   It is merely a reminder to [everyone in] the Universe.

2:93, 12:1, 15:1, 19:74, 24:(1,34,45), 26:1, 27:1, 34:42, 36:(1,69), 43:1, 44:1, 45:24, 57:9, 65:11, 46:6 The chapters and verses in this list all say the same thing: "these are verses from the clear book." Interpreted, this means that the Koran itself says that it should not be difficult to understand the meaning of the passages.

As you can see, the Koran clearly elucidates that it was written so as to be readily understood! But what does it have to say about the issue of interpretation by religious leaders? This subject is discussed in Chapter 9, section 2.

Religious leaders claim that the Koran can only be understood by ordinary people when highly trained clerics interpret it for them. They also say that it is superior to both the Bible and the Torah. My studies have shown me that the Koran is not superior to the books that preceded it, nor a completion of their message, but the reiteration of the message, and that it is a powerful book which should not be adulterated with the views given by men. Read the following extracts of the Koran for yourself and be the judge.

3:2-3 He [God] has sent down the book to you with truth to confirm whatever existed before it. He sent down the Torah and the Gospel in the past as guidance for mankind; He has [also] sent down the standard. Those who disbelieve in God's signs will have severe torment; God is powerful, the master of retribution!

5:52 We have sent you down the book with the truth, to confirm what was already [known] from the [previous] book, and to safeguard it. Judge among them according to what God has sent down, and do not follow their whims concerning any truth that has been given to you. We have given each of you a code of law plus a program [for action].

6:92-93 This is a blessed book [that] We have sent down to confirm whatever came before it, so you may warn the mother of towns and anyone around her. Those who believe in the hereafter believe in it and attend to their prayer. Yet who is more in the wrong than someone who invents a lie about God? Or says: "Something has been revealed to me ..." while nothing has been revealed to him; and who says: "I shall send down the same as God has sent down?" If you could only see when wrongdoers are in their death throes and the angels stretch forth their hands: "Away with your souls! Today you are awarded the torment of shame because you have been saying something that is not true about God. You have acted too proudly for His signs."

10:37 This reading was not invented by anyone except God; but as a confirmation from the Lord of the universe for what He already has and as an analysis of the book which contains no doubt.

12:2 We have sent it down [the Koran] as Arabic reading so that you may reason.

15:10   Truly, We sent [books] down among the sects of early people …

17:79   [Such has been] the practice with any of Our messengers whom We have sent before you. You will never find any change in Our course!

26:193-196 The faithful spirit has descended with it upon your heart that you may be of the warners in plain Arabic language and most surely the same is in the scripture of the ancients.

33:62   [Such is] God's practice with those who have passed on before; you will never find any change in God's practice.

41:43   Anything that has been told you is merely what was told messengers before you. Your God is the master of forgiveness as well as the wielder of painful punishment.

46:11   Before it Moses' book was guidance and blessing. And this book [the Koran] is confirmation in Arabic so it can warn the oppressors and [be] good news for good doers.

87:18-19 This has been [written] on the earliest scrolls, the scriptures of Abraham and Moses.

Once again, there is a clear disparity between that which is said by Moslem religious leaders, and what the Koran has to say about itself. In the Koran, the Torah and the Bible are only spoken about in the most respectful of tones. It is constantly stressed that God's purpose in inspiring the Prophet Muhammad to put His words into writing was to communicate His message to a wider group of people—to speak to the Arab nations in their own language. Now, let's see what the Koran has to say about Arabic and the reason why it was originally written in that language. Moslem clerics insist that Arabic is sacred of itself, and that this is the reason why it was originally used for writing the Koran. They also claim that the Arabic of the Koran is extremely difficult, necessitating a precise knowledge of the language, either as a native speaker or following many years of study. It is stated in the Koran that the use of Arabic was simply intended to allow for easy communication with the Arab people,[6] who did not understand other languages in their region—such as Hebrew—and that the language in the Koran is not particularly difficult. In fact, at no point does there seem to be any ambiguity, and translation from Arabic into modern vernacular languages represents no obstacle to comprehension. Read the following extracts from the Koran and decide for yourself:

6:156-8 This is blessed book We have sent down, so follow it and do your duty so that you may receive mercy, lest you say: "The book was sent down to only two factions before us. We have been unaware of what they study." Or: "If the book had been sent down to us, we would be better guided than they are." Evidence has now come to you from your Lord, as well as guidance and mercy. Who is more in the wrong then someone who rejects God's signs and even evades them? We will reward those who evade Our signs with the worst torment because they have acted thus.

12:2 We have sent it down [the Koran] as [an] Arabic reading so that you may reason.

13:37 And thus have We revealed it, a true judgment in Arabic, and if you follow their low desires after what has come to you in knowledge, you shall not have against God any guardian or a protector.

16:105 … while this is clear Arabic speech.

18:1 Praise be to God, who has sent down the book for His servants and has placed no distortion in it.

26:193-195 The faithful spirit has descended with it upon your heart that you may be of the warners in plain Arabic language.

39:28-29 We have made up every sort of comparison for mankind in this reading so that they may be reminded by an Arabic Koran possessing no ambiguity so that they may do their duty.

41:2 A book whose verses have been spelled out, as an Arabic reading for folk who know.

43:2 We have set it up as an Arabic reading so that you may use your reason.

46:11 Before it Moses' book served as a model and a mercy, while this is a book which confirms [the same message] in the Arabic tongue, so as to warn those who do wrong, and [it forms] an announcement to those who act kindly.

It is also made clear that the Koran is intended to complement, rather than replace or succeed, the Bible and the Torah. This message is stated most clearly in chapter 45, verse 27:

"You will see every nation crouching; each nation will be called before its book: Today you will be rewarded for whatever you have been doing."

Religious leaders who seek to further their own ambitions generally lie about the Koran and say that we should concern ourselves with the *ahadith*—with comments supposedly made by Muhammad or other persons 1400 years ago. Their justification is a line in the Koran that says:

"You must follow God and His prophet."

They extend this to suggest that we should follow everything Muhammad said, whether or not it was inspired by God.

In these circumstances, it is easy for religious leaders to attribute commands with which they agree to figures associated with the origins of Islam. What they forget to tell us is that the Koran tells the stories of many prophets in its various chapters, saying that each time a prophet was appointed, his followers were instructed by God to live according to their message—*during their lifetimes*. However, with the death of each prophet of God comes the contamination of their message until, over centuries, it becomes impossible to sort the truth from the lies.

To live according to the will of God, we must turn instead to His commands in the original texts—the Torah, the Bible and the Koran. It's very simple, but the religious leaders counter by saying that the Koran doesn't instruct Moslems exactly how to live, and that only the *ahadith* can tell them. However, the Koran *does* give instructions for prayer, saying that Moslems should pray five times a day, before sunrise, at noon, in the afternoon, at dusk and at night, and that they should do so in the direction of Kabeh.[7] It also says that Moslems should pray standing or kneeling and bowing to God. In these practices all Moslems are united—but most of the rules associated with praying have no correspondence in the Koran and come, instead, from the teachings of religious leaders.

The *ahadith* vary widely among Moslem populations, especially in the case of the Shiite and the Sunni, and are one of the many sources of conflict between Moslems. Religious leaders do not consider the verses of the Koran that say that there should be unity among men, and that prayer is meaningless when one's actions are not good. True Moslems—those who seek the clarity of God's words instead of following the complex man-made rules called *ahadith*—should always remember that if something is lacking from the Koran, it is because God did not consider it to be sufficiently important to include. To honor God, Moslems should follow the teachings of the Koran, and only those teachings, just as Jews and Christians should live according to the word of God, revealed to them in the Torah and the Bible. Doing so will allow the followers of any of the

holy books to justify to God why they lived the way they did during their
time on Earth.

9.3 Killing in the Koran

Since the attack on America, and the consequent war on terrorism, a
great deal of nonsense has been spoken about what the Koran has to say
about killing, and both Moslem and anti-Moslem apologists have claimed
that the Koran tells its faithful that they should kill innocent human beings
in the name of God. Nothing could be further from the truth.

For centuries, Moslem politicians and religious leaders—who are
often one and the same—have used the Koran to justify the acts they want
their followers to perform. They quote isolated verses out of context,
interpret them as they choose, and tell people that God wants them to kill
for His greater glory. There is no more cunning example of the devil's
works than the misuse of teachings sent to show us how to live with right-
eousness and compassion!

Let me show you how these evil-doers work. Many religious leaders,
including the Ayatollah Khomeni, quote verses like the following:

9:29   Fight those who do not believe in God, nor in the Latter Day, nor
prohibit what God and His apostle have prohibited, nor follow the religion
of truth, out of those who have been given the book, until they pay the tax
in acknowledgement of superiority and they are in a state of subjection.

9:14   Fight them; God will punish them by your hands and bring them
to disgrace, and assist you against them and heal the hearts of a believing
people.

9:124   O you who believe! Fight those of the unbelievers who are near to
you and let them find in you hardness; and know that God is with those
who guard.

47:4   So when you meet in battle those who disbelieve, then smite their
necks until you have overcome them, then make them prisoners, and
afterwards either set them free as a favor or let them ransom until the war
comes to an end. And if God had pleased He would certainly have exacted what is due from them, but that He may try some of you by means of
others; and those who are slain in the way of God, He will by no means
allow their deeds to perish.

By reciting the verses above, these evil-doers persuade young, pure-hearted people—who are usually uneducated about the Koran—to reach a state of extreme excitement, and agree to fight for God. Having achieved this, the evil religious leaders perform the work of the devil to the best of their ability. They quote the verse below, which seals the fate of their followers:

9:112   Surely God has bought of the believers their persons and their property for this, that they shall have the garden; they fight in God's way, so they slay and are slain; a promise which is binding on him in the Torah and the Bible [the New Testament], and the Koran; and who is more faithful to His covenant than God? Rejoice therefore in the pledge which you have made …

All the verses above are taken out of it context. A chapter of the Koran, which is only 6 verses long, is devoted to the topic of non-believers, "The Unbelievers." I quote it in its entirety:

109:1-6   Say: O unbelievers! I do not serve that which you serve, nor do you serve Him Whom I serve: Nor am I going to serve that which you serve, nor are you going to serve Him Whom I serve: You shall have your religion and I shall have my religion.

Another well known verse of the Koran is as follows:

2:257   There is no compulsion in religion; truly the right way has become clearly distinct from the wrong; therefore, whoever disbelieves in Satan and believes in God, he indeed has laid hold of the firmest handle, which shall not break off, and God is hearing, knowing.

It is very clear that God's instruction is to leave non-believers alone. Those verses which instruct Moslems to fight or kill non-believers are invariably either before or after a verse in which it clarifies that these instructions refer specifically to non-believers who are trying to kill them. During the lifetime of the prophet Muhammad, many non-believers and "people of the book" (Jews) tried to destroy him and his followers.

Therefore, when the Koran refers to killing, we must always be careful to read the whole chapter in question, so as to be sure that nothing is taken out of context. Anyone who tries to claim that the Koran says that believers should harm or kill all non-believers is lying. In fact, he is performing the devil's work. The Koran states clearly that it contains no contradictions, and that if it were by anyone other than God, it would contain many.[8] If, then, God repeatedly says that innocent people must not be killed, this must be accepted as His will. Attempts to claim otherwise suggest that the Koran is inconsistent. If the Koran is read by people with pure hearts, they will not fail to see how certain verses are routinely abused by religious leaders. After reading all of the verses in the Koran about killing, I am able to summarize their message as follows:

- Killing aggressors in a just war is permissible.
- One must kill in the way of God.
- One must hurt others to the extent to which one is hurt and no more.
- Do not kill innocent people.
- God's confirmation of peace over war.

After reading all the relevant verses it cannot fail to be seen that the Koran represents a religion of peace, not war. You will also see that the Koran confirms the Bible and the Torah with respect to rules about killing. In contemporary times, these rules are best represented in the United States and other emancipated countries. Unfortunately, none of these nations are Moslem.

9.3.1 Killing in a just war with those who wage war against you

47:4 So when you meet in battle those who disbelieve, then smite their necks until you have overcome them, then make them prisoners, and afterwards either set them free as a favor or let them ransom until the war comes to an end. And if God had pleased He would certainly have exacted what is due from them, but that He may try some of you by means of others; and those who are slain in the way of God, He will by no means allow their deeds to perish.

5:37-39 The penalty for those who wage war on God and His messenger, and spread havoc through the land, is to be slaughtered or crucified, or have their hands and feet cut off on opposite sides, or to be banished from the land. That will mean their disgrace in this world, while they will have serious torment in the hereafter. Except for those who come to terms before you, overpower them. Know that God is forgiving, merciful.

9:3-14 ...and announce painful punishment to those who disbelieve. Except those of the idolaters with whom you made an agreement, then they have not failed you in anything and have not backed up any one against you, so fulfill their agreement to the end of their term; surely God loves those who are careful (of their duty). So when the sacred months have passed away, then slay the idolaters wherever you find them, and take them captive and besiege them and lie in wait for them in every ambush, then if they repent and keep up prayer and pay the poor-rate, leave their way free to them; sure-ly God is forgiving, merciful. And if one of the idolaters seek protection from you, grant him protection till he hears the word of God, then make him attain his place of safety; this is because they are a people who do not know. How can there be an agreement for the idolaters with God and with His messenger; except those with whom you made an agreement at the Sacred Mosque. So as long as they are true to you, be true to them; surely God loves those who are careful [of their duty]. How [can it be]! While if they prevail against you, they would not pay regard in your case to ties of relationship, nor those of covenant; they please you with their mouths while their hearts do not consent; and most of them are transgressors. They have taken a small price for the communications of God, so they turn away from His way; sure-ly evil is it that they do. They do not pay regard to ties of relationship nor those of covenant in the case of a believer; and these are they who go beyond the limits. But if they repent and keep up prayer and pay the poor rate, they are your brethren in faith; and We make the communications clear for a peo-ple who know. And if they break their oaths after their agreement and [open-ly] revile your religion, then fight the leaders of unbelief—surely their oaths are nothing—so that they may desist. What! Will you not fight a people who broke their oaths and aimed at the expulsion of the messenger, and they attacked you first; do you fear them? But God is most deserving that you should fear Him, if you are believers. Fight them; God will punish them by your hands and bring them to disgrace, and assist you against them and heal the hearts of a believing people.

9:36   Surely the number of months with God is twelve months in God's ordinance since the day when He created the Heavens and the Earth, of these four being sacred; that is the right reckoning; therefore be not unjust to yourselves regarding them, and fight the polytheists all together as they fight you all together; and know that God is with those who guard [against evil].

49:9   And if two parties of the believers quarrel, make peace between them; but if one of them acts wrongfully towards the other, fight that which acts wrongfully until it returns to God's command; then if it returns, make peace between them with justice and act equitably; surely God loves those who act equitably.

2:212-213 Fighting is also prescribed for you even though it may seem detestable to you. It may be that you detest something which is good for you; while perhaps you love something even though it is bad for you. God knows, while you do not know.

4:93   You will find others who desire that they should be safe from you and secure from their own people; whenever they are sent back to the mischief they get thrown into it headlong; therefore if they do not withdraw from you, and offer you peace and restrain their hands, then seize them and kill them wherever you find them; and against these We have given you a clear authority.

8:40   And fight with them until there is no more persecution and religion should be only for God; but if they desist, then surely God sees what they do.

2:214   They will ask you about fighting during the hallowed month. Say: "Fighting in it is serious, while obstructing God's way, disbelief in Him and the hallowed mosque, and turning His people out of it are even more serious with God. Even dissension's more serious than killing." They will never stop fighting you until they make you abandon your religion if they can manage to do so. Anyone who abandons his religion and dies while he is a disbeliever will find their actions will miscarry in this world and the hereafter. Those [will become] inmates of the fire; they will remain there.

9.3.2   Kill in the way of God

22:40   Permission is given to those upon whom war is made because they are oppressed, and most surely God is well able to assist them.

4:76-78 Therefore let those fight in the way of God, who sell this world's life for the hereafter; and whoever fights in the way of God, then be he slain or be he victorious, We shall grant him a mighty reward. And what reason have you that you should not fight in the way of God and of the weak among the men and the women and the children, those who say:

"Our Lord! Cause us to go forth from this town, whose people are oppressors, and give us from Thee a guardian and give us from Thee a helper. Those who believe fight in the way of God, and those whose disbelieve fight in the way of the devil. Fight therefore against the friends of Satan, surely the strategy of Satan is weak.

4:86   Fight them in God's way; this is not imposed on you except in relation to yourself. And rouse the believers to ardor; maybe God will restrain the fighting of those who disbelieve, and God is strongest in prowess and strongest in giving an exemplary punishment.

2:245   Fight in God's way and know that God is alert, aware.

3:161   And that He might know the hypocrites; and it was said to them: Come, fight in God's way, or defend yourselves. They said: "If we knew fighting, we would certainly have followed you. They were on that day much nearer to disbelief than to belief. They say with their mouths what is not in their hearts; and God best knows what they conceal."

9:112   Surely God has bought of the believers their persons and their property for this, that they shall have the garden; they fight in God's way, so they slay and are slain; a promise which is binding on him in the Torah and the Bible [the New Testament], and the Koran; and who is more faithful to His covenant than God? Rejoice therefore in the pledge which you have made …

9.3.3   Hurt them as much as they hurt you and no more

2:190   One forbidden month matches another forbidden month, while sacred matters have means of compensation. Attack him to the same extent to which he has attacked you. Heed God, and know that God stands by the heedful.

2:173   You who believe, compensation for murder has been prescribed for you: the freeman for the free, the slave for the slave, and the female for the female. Anyone who is pardoned in any way for it by his brother should follow this appropriately, and handsomely make amends with him; that means a lightening as well as mercy from your Lord. Anyone who exceeds the limit after that shall have painful torment.

9.3.4 Do not kill innocent people

25:68 And they who do not call upon another god with God and do not slay the soul, which God has forbidden except in the requirements of justice, and do not commit fornication. He who does this shall find a requital of sin.

17:35 And do not kill anyone whom God has forbidden except for a just cause. Whoever is slain unjustly, We have indeed given to His heir authority, so let him not exceed the just limits in slaying; surely he is aided.

6:152 Say: "Come, I will recite what your God has forbidden to you, that you do not associate anything with Him and show kindness to your parents, and do not slay your children for poverty. We provide for you and for them, and do not draw nigh to indecencies, those which are apparent and those which are concealed, and do not kill the soul which God has forbidden except for the requirements of justice; this He has enjoined you with in hope that you learn from it."

4:91 They desire that you should disbelieve as they have disbelieved, so that you might be alike; therefore take not from among them friends until they move in God's way; but if they turn back, then seize them and kill them wherever you find them, and take not from among them a friend or a helper.

4:92 Except those who joined a people with whom you have an alliance, or who come to you, their hearts shrinking from fighting you or fighting their own people; and if God had pleased, He would have given them power over you, so that they should have certainly fought you; therefore if they withdraw from you and do not fight you and offer you peace, then God has not given you a way against them.

4:33 You who believe, do not use up your wealth idly, on one another, unless it is for some business based on mutual consent among you. Do not kill one another; God has been merciful towards you!

4:94 And it does not behoove a believer to kill a believer except by mistake, and whoever kills a believer by mistake should free a believing slave, and blood-money should be paid to his people unless they remit it as alms; but if he be from a tribe hostile to you and he is a believer ... and if he is from a tribe between whom and you there is a covenant, the blood-money should be paid to his people along with the freeing of a believing slave; but he who cannot find [the money] should fast for two months successively: a penance from God, and God is knowing, wise.

4:95   And whoever kills a believer intentionally, his punishment is Hell; he shall abide in it, and God will send His wrath on him and curse him and prepare for him a painful chastisement.

5:33   Then his mind facilitated to him the slaying of his brother, so he slew him; then he became one of the losers.

5:35   For this reason did we prescribe to the children of Israel that whoever slays a soul, unless it be for manslaughter or for mischief in the land, it is as though he slew all men; and whoever keeps it alive, it is as though he kept alive all men; and certainly Our apostles came to them with clear arguments, but even after that many of them certainly act extravagantly in the land.

9.3.5   God's confirmation that peace should prevail war

60:8   God does not forbid you from respecting those who have not made war against you on account of [your] religion, and have not driven you forth from your homes, that you show them kindness and deal with them justly; surely God loves the doers of justice.

60:9   God only forbids you from respecting those who made war upon you on account of religion, and drove you forth from your homes and backed up your expulsion, that you make friends with them, and whoever makes friends with them, these are the unjust.

Taken together, the verses above clearly say that unless war is waged against us in the name of religion, or enemies try to force us from our homes, we have no reason to kill. Sadly, verses such as 60:8-9 are rarely cited by Moslem religious leaders, and the reason why is as obvious as it is depressing; teachings which promote peace and compassion are not compatible with terrorist acts, or with teaching hatred of people of other nations.

Moreover, all the verses about killing clearly state that those who wage war against believers should be punished—while God makes it clear that those who accept peace should not be hurt. Ayatollah Khomeni and similar leaders quote the Koran and reach conclusions such as:
"You should fight America with no fear, as God has promised in the

Koran that whether you die or are victorious in battle you are the winner." This sort of abuse of the Koran's verses is very common. Of course, those who speak of America in such a way are unable to specify what America's crime is. In fact, as you can see from reading the verses in the Koran which refer to killing, America fulfills none of the criteria for justifiable war as described by God.

Do the Americans or the American government try to stop believers from believing in God? No.

Do they try to evict people from their homes? Again, no.

But in the Koran, God tells us that we must only fight in self-defense! How could the recent attacks on American embassies around the world, and on America, be classified as acts of self-defense?

The idea of pitting themselves against a powerful nation like America is fashionable among young Moslem men who seek glory, and look to their religious leaders for guidance. Few of these youths listen to the less "glamorous" message of the Koran—that he who studies and does his best to improve his intellect is beloved of God. How much more tedious it is to study so that their countries can develop to the full extent of their potential than to blame America for their own shortcomings! Tragically, these young men, who are more hot-blooded than sensible, are easily led by authority figures such as Khomeni, who has said:

"Whatever problems you [the Iranian people] experience, blame them on no one but America."

In the Koran, it states that we can only blame ourselves for the hardships we suffer.[9] God created human beings so that they would develop their powers of thought and reason to the full extent of their ability. To follow the laws of God, religious leaders should urge those who listen to them to study and think for themselves—not to blame America whenever anything goes wrong.

9.4 What does the Koran have to say about who will go to Heaven?

Moslem religious leaders, like the leaders of every type of religious group, maintain that those who do not think exactly as they do cannot be saved. Conveniently, this makes their followers dependent on them for salvation. The Koran preaches a very different message, however, saying that the person who believes in God and does good deeds is guaranteed a place in Heaven. The simplicity of this message does not accord well with the religious leaders. Shiite Moslems especially insist that salvation can only be found through their belief system—as is also the case with those who subscribe to other belief systems, although the repercussions of their insistence are usually more serious. The shocking truth of the matter is that the religious leaders of Islam are lying about the issue of salvation, as they do about so much more. Read the extracts below and judge for yourself.

2:23   And give the good news to those who believe in God and do good deeds, they will have Heaven that has rivers in it …..

2:76   Those who are believers and do good deeds, they belong to Heaven and they will be there forever.

3:50   Those who are believers and do good deeds, God will give their reward fully …

4:60   And those who are believers and do good deeds, we will bring them into Heaven that has in it rivers and they will be there forever …

4:123   Those who believe in God, whether male or female, and do good deeds, then they will enter Heaven.

4:172   Those who are believers and do good deeds, then [God] will give their rewards fully …

5:12   God has given them a promise that if they are believers and do good deeds, for them there is great reward…[10]

The Koran states more than fifty-five times that those who have faith in God and do good will go to Heaven. It seems that God is striving to emphasize the simplicity of His command. It is also interesting to note that nowhere does it say that Moslems will be given preference in the afterlife. However, it does say:

"Truly those who have faith (in this prophet) and the Jews, and those who are changing their religion from one to another, and those Christians, whoever has faith in God and does good deeds, then there is no fear for them and they will never be saddened."[11]

In spite of this, religious leaders have taught that the only way to God is their way. They make simple things seem complex, and teach their people that they are superior to all others. They say that the Koran says that people should do good deeds, but that people need their help to know what a good deed is. Although civilized men and women, living in the modern world, should need no explanation of the difference between good and evil, we all need to be reminded to do good! The Koran was written at a time when simple, unsophisticated tribal society was the norm and definitions of good deeds were provided for the fledgling faithful. The following verse describes God's definition of doing good:

2:172   Doing good is not just facing west or east, but a good-doer is the one who believes in God and the last day and the angels and the book and the prophets, and gives away wealth out of love for Him to the near of kin and the orphans and the needy and the one that is passing by and the one that is in need of help and the one who asks for help and the captives, and one who prays and pays tithes [a proportion of one's income, set aside for the poor], and the performers of their promise when they make a promise, and the patient in hard times and affliction and in time of conflicts, these are they who are true to themselves and these are the real believers.

23:3-11 ...those who are humble in their prayers and who keep aloof from what is vain and who are givers of tithes to the poor and who guard their private parts except before their spouses ... and those who are keepers of their trusts and their covenant and those who guard their prayers.

In no way can these verses be thought to justify the multi-layered rules of modern Islam. Clearly, they were intended to be simple, and to be understood. God made humankind intelligent enough to build the world we see around us—I'm sure He trusts us to comprehend His most basic commands. However, the purest of messages have become corrupted by the workings of Islamic religious leaders, and it is their pride that leads them to promote hatred so much that the word of God becomes twisted until it can truly be said to represent the word of the devil and all his works. This is the perverse process that leads to the existence of terrorism, hate and destruction.

9.5 What does the Koran have to say about religious leaders?

This is indeed a fascinating topic. The recurring theme of this book is that religion has been distorted by the very religious leaders whose duty it should be to help us to live well. In fact, the Koran and the Bible both describe encounters between God's prophets and the religious leaders of their day. During one encounter with the Jewish religious leaders, Jesus said:

"The blood of all the prophets which was shed from the foundation of the world may be required of this generation, from the blood of Abel to the blood of Zachariah who perished between the altar and the temple. Yes, I say to you, it shall be required of your generation [all the religious leaders as whole]."[12]

It is interesting to compare the actions of modern religious leaders with the actions of historical religious leaders during the times of Jesus and Muhammad. When Jesus stated that he spent time with the sick and the needy, with drunks and prostitutes, because these were the people who needed him most, he was met with scorn. The Jewish religious leaders of those days disdained him and wished him dead. Jesus was able to bring many people to salvation, but the ones who were beyond help were the very religious leaders who were considered by themselves and others to be above reproach. Today, a similar situation prevails, especially in Moslem nations. Let's examine what the Koran itself has to say about religious leaders:

2:38-9 …Do not sell God's words for any price … and do not mix up the truth with the falsehood, nor hide the truth while you know it.

2:56 But those who did injustice by changing the word [of God] to another word which had been spoken to them, so We send down to those who did this injustice a punishment from the sky because they transgressed.

2:70 Do you then wish that they would believe in you, and a group of them indeed heard the word of God, then altered it after they had understood it, and they know [this].

2:73 And there are among them illiterates who know not the book but only lies, and they are of all doubts, therefore woe, to those who write the book with their hands and then say: "This is from God, so that they may take for it a small price; therefore woe to them for what their hands have written and woe to them for what they earn from it."

2:134 …Who is more unjust than someone who hides some evidence from God which He holds?…

2:141 …Nevertheless a group of them hide the truth even though they know it.

2:154-155 God curses those who hide whatever We send down as explanations and guidance, once We have explained it to mankind in the book, and cursers will cure them. Except for those who repent, and explain [what they hide from people]…

2:164 He [the devil] merely orders you to commit evil and shocking deeds, and to say what you do not know about God.

2:169-171 Those who hide what God has sent down in the book and sell it for a small worldly price. They do not eat but the fire in their bellies. God will not speak to them on the Resurrection Day nor will He purify them; they will have painful torment! Those are the ones who have purchased error instead of guidance, and torment instead of forgiveness. Why do they insist on facing the fire? That is because God has sent the book down with the truth, while those who disagree about the book go much too far in dissension.[13]

3:57 Say: "People of the book, rally to a common formula to be binding on both us and you, that we shall worship only God and associate nothing else with Him, nor shall any of us take on others as lords instead of God, if they disagree tell them be witness that we are Moslems."

3:71 Those who take small price for the covenant of God and their own oaths, surely they shall have no portion in the hereafter, and God will not speak to them, nor will He look upon them on the Day of Resurrection nor will He purify them, and they shall have a painful chastisement.

3:72 Most surely there is a group among those who distort the book with their tongue that you may consider it to be part of the book, and they say, "It is from God," while it is not from God; and they tell a lie against God while they know.

3:184 And when God made a covenant with those who were given the book: You shall certainly make it known to men and you shall not hide it; but they cast it behind their backs and took a small price for it; so evil is that which they buy.

5:48 We have sent down the Torah containing guidance and light. The prophets who were committed to live in peace judge those who were Jews by means of it, and the rabbis and scholars must guard the book of God and be witness for it. So do not dread mankind, and dread Me; do not buy up My signs for a worldly price. Those who do not judge by what

God has sent down are disbelievers!

6:21   Yet who is more in the wrong than someone who invents a lie about God, or has rejected His signs? Wrongdoers will never prosper.

6:93   Yet who is more in the wrong than someone who invents a lie about God? Or says: "Something has been revealed to me …" while nothing has been revealed to him; and who says: "I shall send down the same as God has sent down." If you could only see when wrongdoers are in their death throes and the angels stretch forth their hands. Away with your souls! Today you are awarded the torment of shame because you have been saying something that is not true about God. You have acted too proudly …

6:123   And thus have We made in every town the great ones to be its guilty ones, that they may plan therein; and they do not plan but against their own souls, and they do not perceive.

9:31   They have adopted their scholars and monks as lords instead of God …

9:34-35 You who believe, many scholars and monks do consume people's wealth to no good purpose and they obstruct God's way. Announce painful torment to those who hoard gold and silver and do not spend them for God's sake. On the day when it shall be heated in the fire of Hell, then their foreheads and their sides and their backs shall be branded with it; this is what you hoarded up for yourselves, therefore taste what you hoarded.

10:69   Say: "Truly those who invent a lie about God will never prosper."

11:20   Yet who is more in the wrong than someone who invents a lie about God?

26:197   There is no verse for them unless the scholars from the children of Israel knew about it.

29:68   Who is more in the wrong than someone who invents a lie about God and rejects the truth even when it has come to him? Will there not be room in Hell for disbelievers?

31:5   Some men buy up vain words to mislead from God's way without having any knowledge, and they take it as a joke. They shall have shameful torment.

39:33   Who is more in the wrong than someone who lies about God and denies the facts even though they come to him? Is there not room in Hell for such disbelievers?

40:37   Those who dispute concerning the signs of God, without any authority, are very hateful in the sight of God and the believers; so God sets a seal on every proud and arrogant heart.

40:58   Those who dispute concerning the signs of God, without any authority, in their breasts is only pride, that they shall never attain. So seek thou refuge in God; surely He is the all-hearing, the all-seeing.

61:7   …and what is a greater evil than he who forges falsehood against God…

61:8   [They] desire to extinguish with their mouths the light of God; but God will perfect His light, though the unbelievers are averse.

It is fair to assume that, considering the damage that religious leaders have wrought on society, God would address this issue in His holy book. In His omniscience, He must have known that religious leaders would use their authority to evil ends, creating monsters of human beings. The rabbis, priests and ayatollahs of the world should use their authority to remind us to do God's work, and not the devil's. They should teach the word of God. Instead, we have in the *resalah* the prime example of man's laws being given more prominence than those of God. I beseech Moslems everywhere to put aside their customary hatred and prejudice and learn to understand the law of God as it has been recorded in the Koran.

9.6 What does the Koran say about Moslems?

The word "Moslem" has been lifted from the Koran by religious leaders, and applied exclusively to a particular group of people with no justification whatsoever. In the Koran, "Moslem" is used to describe all believers, including Jews, Christians and the followers of Islam:

"Your forefather, Abraham, first named you Moslems."[14]

The Koran, as the most recent of the great religious texts, has been the least subject to contamination, so let's see what that great book has to say about the identity of those people properly referred to as "Moslem:"

2:122   Our Lord, allow us two [Abraham and Ishmael] to be Moslems, and make our offspring into a nation which is Moslem. Show us our ceremonies and turn towards us. You are so relenting, the merciful!

2:126   Abraham commissioned his sons with it, and Jacob: "My sons, God has selected your religion for you. Do not die unless you are Moslems."

2:127   Or were you present as death appeared for Jacob, when he said to his sons: "What will you serve after I am gone?" They said: "We shall worship your God and the God of your forefathers Abraham, Ishmael, and Isaac: God Alone! We are Moslems."

2:130   Say: "We believe in God and what has been sent down to us, and what was sent down to Abraham, Ishmael, Isaac, Jacob and their descendants, and what was given Moses and Jesus, and what was given the prophets by their Lord. We do not discriminate against any one of them and are Moslems."

3:17   Religion with God means Islam, a commitment to peace. Those who have already been given the book did not disagree until after knowledge had come to them, out of envy for one another. Anyone who disbelieves in God's signs, God is prompt in reckoning!

Here we see an explicit definition of Islam: "a commitment to peace."

3:18   If they should argue with you, then say: "I have committed myself peacefully to God, and so has anyone who follows me." Tell both who have been given the book [Jews and Christians] as well as the unlettered [those who don't have a book from God]: "Have you become Moslems?" If they commit themselves to peace, then they are guided; while if they turn away, you merely need to state things plainly. God is observant of worshippers.

Here we see God saying: "If you are committed to peace then you are guided and therefore you are Moslem."

3:45   When Jesus sensed disbelief among them, he said: "Who will be my supporters in the cause of God?" The disciples said: "We are God's supporters! We believe in God; take note that we are Moslems."

3:57   Say: "People of the book, [Jews and Christians] let us rally to a common formula to be binding on both us and you, that we shall worship only God and associate nothing else with Him, nor shall any of us take on others as lords instead of God." If they should turn away, then say: "Bear witness that we are Moslems."

A common theme in the Koran, God's plea that all people should become Moslem, is expressed here as: " … that we shall worship only God and associate nothing else with Him, nor shall any of us take on others as lords instead of God." The movement initiated by the Prophet Muhammad was intended to unite all of those who believe in God. Sadly, this has never happened.

3:60 Abraham was neither a Jew nor a Christian, but he was a seeker of truth, a Moslem; he was no associator of others with God.

3:74 He does not order you to adopt angels and prophets as lords; would he order you to disbelieve once you have become a Moslem [a believer]?"

3:77 Do they crave something besides God's religion? Whoever is in Heaven and Earth is Moslem [committed to peace] for Him, whether willingly or reluctantly; to Him will they be returned.

Everything in nature obeys a set of rules created by God, and God says that everything in Heaven and on Earth is Moslem, or submitted to God. Clearly, a Moslem is a person who has submitted him or herself to God.

3:78 Say: "We believe in God and what has been sent down to us, and what was sent down to Abraham, Ishmael, Isaac, Jacob and their descendants, and what was given to Moses, Jesus, and the prophets by their Lord. We do not differentiate between any one of them, and we are Moslem [committed to peace] with Him."

3:79 Anyone who desires something other than commitment to peace [Islam] as a religion will never have it accepted from Him, while in the hereafter he will be among the losers.

3:97 You who believe, heed God the way He should be heeded, and do not die unless you are Moslems.

4:124 Who is finer in religion than someone who peacefully commends himself to God [a Moslem] while he acts kindly and follows the sect of Abraham the inquirer? God adopted Abraham as a bosom friend.

5:5 Today I have perfected your religion for you, and completed My favor towards you, and have consented to grant you Islam as a religion: a commitment to live in peace.

5:111   When I inspired the disciples [of Jesus] to believe in Me and in My messenger, they said: "We believe, so take witness that we are Moslems."

6:163   No associate has He, with that am I commanded, and I am the first of the Moslems.

7:123   You are persecuting us only because we have believed in our Lord's signs once they were brought us. Our Lord, pour patience over us, and gather us up at death as Moslems!

10:72   So should you turn away, I have not asked you for any payment; my payment comes only from God, and I have been ordered to become a Moslem.

10:84   Moses said: "My people, if you believe in God, then rely on Him if you are Moslems."

10:90   So we brought the children of Israel across the sea. Pharaoh and his armies had them followed in hot pursuit and fought them off until, as drowning overtook him, he said: "I believe that there is no deity except the one whom the children of Israel believe in. I am now a Moslem."

Here we see that, by accepting God, Pharaoh considers himself a Moslem—even though this acceptance only occurred at the moment of his death. Could it possibly be clearer that the term "Moslem" simply indicates "belief in God?"

11:16   If they do not respond to you, then know it has only been sent down with God's knowledge. There is no deity except Him. Will you not become Moslems?"

12:102   [The Prophet Joseph says] "My Lord, you have given me control and taught me how to interpret events. Originator of Heaven and Earth, you are my patron in this world and the hereafter. Gather me in as a Moslem and unite me with honorable men!"

15:2   Perhaps those who disbelieve would like to become Moslems.

16:91   Someday We shall raise up a witness from every nation against them from among themselves. We shall even bring you as a witness against such persons. We have sent the book down to you to explain everything, and for guidance and mercy, and as good news for Moslems.

16:104 Say: "The Holy Spirit has brought it down as truth from your Lord to brace those who believe, and as guidance and good news for Moslems."

Again, God refers to those who believe as "Moslems."

21:108 Say: "It has only been revealed to me that your God is God Alone. Are you Moslem?"

Here it is once more clear that the person who believes in God is a Moslem.

22:77 Strive for God's sake, the way He should be striven for. He has picked you out and has not placed any constraint upon you concerning religion, the sect of your forefather Abraham. He has named you Moslems both previously and right now, so the messenger may be a witness for you, and you may act as witnesses for mankind. Keep up prayer and pay the welfare tax, and cling firmly to God; He is your protector. What a splendid protector, and what a splendid supporter!

27:31 Do not act haughtily towards me, and come to me as a Moslem.

27:38 He [the Prophet Solomon] said: "Councilman, which of you will bring me her throne before they come to me as a Moslem?"

27:83 You are no one to guide the blind from their error; you will only cause someone who believes in Our verses to listen, for they are Moslems.

27:93 I have only been ordered to serve the Lord of this region which He has hallowed. He possesses everything. I have been ordered to be a Moslem.

28:53 Whenever it is recited to them, they say: "We believe in it; it is the truth from our Lord! We have already been Moslems."

29:45 Do not argue with the people of the book [Jews and Christians] unless it is in the politest manner, except for those among them who do wrong. Say: "We believe in what has been sent down to us and what has been sent down to you. Our God and your God is One, and we are Moslems."

30:52 You are no one to guide the blind from their error: only someone who believes in Our verses will listen; since they are Moslems.

39:14 I have been ordered to be the first of those who are Moslems.

41:33   Who speaks in a finer way than someone who appeals to God, acts honorably and says: "I am a Moslem!"

43:69   Those who believe in Our signs and are Moslems:

46:14   We have instructed every man to be kind to both his parents. His mother bears him with reluctance, and gives birth to him painfully. Bearing him and weaning him last thirty months, until when he attains his full growth and reaches forty years, he says: "My Lord, train me to be grateful for Your favor which you have shown to me and to both my parents, and to act honorably so You may approve of it. Improve my offspring for me: I have turned toward You and am one of those who are Moslems."

51:36   [God cursed and destroyed all Prophet Lot's tribe] except We found only one house with Moslems in it.

68:35   Are We to treat Moslems as if they are sinners?

72:14   Some of us are Moslems while others of us are holding back. Those who are Moslems are dedicated to integrity.

Reading the above verses, it is painfully clear that the leaders of Islam have appropriated the word "Moslem" and used it only for themselves instead of passing on the message of the Koran—the same message that reverberates through the ages through the prophets of God. The word "Moslem" should, instead, be used to describe all of those who believe in God, including those who, like Pharaoh in verse 10:90, mentioned above, come to God just moments before death.

Most of the inhabitants of this world believe in God. If they recognized their commonality, the Earth's economy and state of being would be altered beyond recognition. Nations and the people who inhabit them would be applauded for their achievements and no believer would hate another, simply because of minor differences in traditional practices of worship. All would be believers—all would be Moslem, in the true and original meaning of the word.

9.7 What does the Koran have to say about Christians and Jews?

During the lifetime of the Prophet Muhammad, there were many conflicts between Moslems, Christians and Jews, and the Koran addresses the situations that arise from these problems. Don't forget that the

Bible also deals with Jesus' dismissal of the Jewish religious leaders of his day, when he denounces their corruption, and their tendency to put the laws of man before the laws of God.

In the Koran, the subject of the relationship between members of these three great faiths is discussed in some detail, stressing the essential sameness of the message sent by God to these groups—it even says explicitly that it "contains nothing new"[15] but simply reiterates the simple message that humanity should love God and do good. It also mentions the damage done over the years to sincere believers of any denomination by corrupt religious leaders.

All of the information contained in the Koran about the corruption of Jewish and Christian religious authorities is of utmost importance, as it enlightens us as to the later corruption of Islam by its religious leaders. In the extracts from the Koran quoted below, it is clear that the laws of the Koran are the very same as those in the Bible and the Torah. They are God's laws, and God's laws, quite simply, do not change.

God has always wanted humankind to love each other, to love Him, and to do good. For example, in chapter 41, verse 32, the Koran says that we should react to those who would do us harm with kindness, and love our enemies as if they were our closest friends. This verse should be compulsory reading for all those who kill in the name of religion. Now, Moslem religious leaders are very familiar with this particular verse. On one occasion, when I was listening to a Koran reading at a mosque, I was surprised by how the religious leader in question rushed through this verse, mumbling, as if God had been in error when He made that particular instruction.

The verses below are quoted according to six separate subcategories, as follows:

❖ The argument among Jews, Christians, and Moslems about who is right and who is wrong.

❖ The story of Jesus Christ as revealed in the Koran.

❖ God's plea that Jews, Christians and Moslems should live in unity.

❖ Praise for Jews and Christians in the Koran.

❖ The Koran's teaching that the only difference between Christians and Moslems is the Christian belief in Christ as the son of God.

❖ The Koran's insistence that Christians should uphold the Bible and Jews should uphold the Torah.

9.7.1   The argument among Jews, Christians, and Moslems about who is right and who is wrong

2:107   Jews say: "Christians have no point to make" while Christians say: "The Jews have no point to make" yet they [all] quote from the [same] book. Likewise those who do not know anything make a statement similar to theirs. God will judge between them on the Resurrection Day concerning how they have been differing.

2:254   We have preferred some messengers over others. Some of them God spoke to, while others He raised in rank. We gave Jesus the son of Mary explanations, and endorsed him by means of the Holy Spirit. If God had wished, the ones who came after them would not have fallen out with one another once explanations had come to them; however, they disagreed. Some of them believed while others disbelieved. If God had wished, they would not have fallen out with one another, but God does whatever He wants.

In the verses above, God makes it clear that, had He wished, He could have united people of all different religions Himself, but chose instead to let them follow the dictates of their own conscience.

3:58-61 People of the book, why do you argue about Abraham when the Torah and the Bible were not sent down until after him? Do you not use your reason? There you go, arguing on about someone you have some knowledge about! Yet why do you argue about something you have no knowledge about? God knows while you do not know. Abraham was neither a Jew nor a Christian, but he was a seeker of truth, a Moslem (as were Jesus, and Moses); he was no associator. The closest people to Abraham are those who follow him, as well as this prophet and those who believe. God is the believers' patron.

3:63   People of the book, why do you disbelieve in God's signs while you watch them happen?

These pleas were made at a time when God wished earnestly for the people to follow the teachings revealed through the Prophet Muhammad. The emphasis on the essential sameness of Jews, Christians and Moslems cannot be mistaken—nor can the use of the term "Moslem" simply to denote "believer."

3:64   People of the book, why do you dress truth up with falsehood and knowingly conceal it?

The above verse refers to religious leaders who behave as if they were teaching the people about God's laws but who actually change the laws beyond recognition. They make falsehood look like truth. This is what happened in the times of Muhammad, and this is what still occurs today. Well-meaning men and women are thus encouraged to live according to harmful laws that have no basis in God's teachings. For example, Moslem religious leaders tell their followers that if they want to die as martyrs, they must fight God's enemies and die for Him. Most often, the leaders describe God's enemies as the Americans. And unfamiliar as the Moslems are with the real message of God as it is revealed in the Koran, too many take such instructions seriously.

3:96   How can you disbelieve while God's verses are being recited to you and His messenger is among you? Anyone who clings to God will be guided to a straight road.

The verse above clearly indicates that those who heard the words of God as spoken by His prophet and still disbelieve are much more culpable that those who never heard, and do not understand.

4:122   It is not up to what you wish [Muhammad's followers], nor up to what the people of the book [Jews and Christians] wish. Anyone who commits evil will be rewarded accordingly and not find any patron nor protector for himself besides God.

In this simple verse lies the most powerful, potent answer to the most difficult question posed by religion: How can one be saved? It is immediately clear that what really matters is not whether one attends a mosque, or a synagogue, or a church, but whether or not one lives well and does good. Ultimately, it doesn't matter whether you stand or kneel to pray, cover your hair or take off your shoes. What really concerns God is the way you lead your life, and that you strive to do His will.

9.7.2   The story of Christ in the Koran

Many don't realize that Jesus Christ is recognized as an important prophet of God in the Koran, but this is very much the case, as the vers es below demonstrate:

3:31-44 Thus a woman [descended from] Imron said: "My Lord, I have freely consecrated whatever is in my womb to You. Accept it from me; You are alert, aware!" When she gave birth, she said: "My Lord, I have given birth to a daughter. I have named her Mary, and ask You to protect her and her offspring from Satan the outcast." Her Lord accepted her in a handsome manner and caused her to grow like a lovely plant and told Zachariah to take care of her. Every time Zachariah entered the shrine to see her, he found she had already been supplied with food. He said: "Mary, how can this be meant for you?" She said: "It comes from God, for God provides for anyone He wishes without any reckoning." With that Zachariah appealed to His Lord; saying: "My Lord, grant me goodly offspring from Your presence, for You are the Hearer of Appeals." The angels called him while he was standing praying in the shrine: "God gives you news of John, who will confirm word from God, masterful yet circumspect, and a prophet from among honorable people." He said: "My Lord, how can I have a boy? Old age has overtaken me, while my wife is barren." He said: "Even so does God do anything He wishes!" He said: "My Lord, grant me a sign." He said: "Your sign is that you will not speak to people for three days except through gestures. Mention your Lord often and glorify Him in the evening and early morning hours." So the angels said: "Mary, God has selected you and purified you. He has selected you over the women in the Universe. Mary, devote yourself to your Lord; fall down on your knees and bow alongside those so bow down." Such is the information about the unseen we have revealed to you. You were not in their presence as they cast their pens to see which of them would be entrusted with Mary. You were not in their presence while they were so disputing. Thus the angels said: "Mary, God announces word to you about someone whose name will be Christ Jesus, the son of Mary, who is well regarded in this world and the hereafter, and one of those drawn near. He will speak to people while still an infant and as an adult, and will be an honorable person." She said: "My Lord, how can I have a child while no human being has ever touched me?" He said: "That is how God creates anything He wishes. Whenever He decides upon some matter, He merely tells it: "Be!" and it is. He will teach him the book and wisdom, and the Torah and the Bible. As a messenger to the Children of Israel: "I have brought you a sign from your Lord. I shall create something in the shape of a bird for you out of clay, and blow into it so it will become a real bird with God's permission. I shall cure those who are blind from birth and lepers, and revive the dead with God's permission. I shall announce to you what you may eat and what you should store up in your houses. That will serve as a sign for you if you are believers, confirming what I have already learned from the Torah. I shall permit you some things which have been forbidden you. I have brought you a sign from your Lord, so heed God and obey me! God is both my Lord and your Lord, so serve Him. This is a straight road!"

2:254 We have preferred some messengers over others. Some of them God spoke to, while others He raised in rank. We gave Jesus the son of Mary explanations, and endorsed him by means of the Holy Spirit. If God had wished, the ones who came after them would not have fallen out with one another once explanations had come to them; however they disagreed. Some of them believed while others disbelieved. If God had wished, they would not have fallen out with one another, but God does whatever He wants.

Moslem religious leaders claim that Muhammad was the greatest prophet ever sent. If this was true, then God would have stated so in the Koran. Instead, when God talks of a prophet being greater than others, the name He mentions is that of Jesus.

3:52 Jesus' [origin] with God was the same as Adam's: He created him from dust: then told him: "Be!" and he was.

19:16-41 Mention in the book how Mary withdrew from her people to an Eastern place. She chose to be secluded from them. We sent her Our spirit, who presented himself to her as a full–grown human being. She said: "Take refuge with the mercy-giving from you, unless you are someone who does his duty." He said: "I am only your Lord's messenger to bestow a clean-living boy on you." She said: "How shall I have a boy when no human being has ever touched me, nor am I a loose woman?" He said: "Thus your Lord has said: "It is a simple matter for Me. We will grant him as a sign for mankind and a mercy from Ourselves. It is a matter that has been decided." So she conceived him, and withdrew to a remote place to have him. Labor pains came over her by the trunk of a date palm. She said: "If only I had died before this, and been forgotten, overlooked!" Someone called out to her from below where she was: "Don't feel so sad! Your Lord has placed a brook at your feet. Shake the trunk of the date palm towards you so it will drop some fresh dates on you. Eat and drink, and refresh yourself. Should you see even a single human being, then say: 'I have vowed to keep a fast to the Mercy-giving whereby I'll never speak to any person today!'" She carried him back to her family. They said: "Mary, you have brought something hard to believe! Kinswoman of Aaron, your father was no evil man, nor was your mother a loose woman." She pointed to him. They said: "How shall we talk to someone who is a child in the cradle?" He said: "I am God's servant. He has given me the book and made me a prophet. He has made me blessed wherever I may be, and commissioned me to pray and [pay] the welfare tax so long as I live, and to act with consideration towards my mother. He has not made me domineering, hard to get along with. Peace be on the day I was born, and the day I shall die and the day I am raised to life again!" Such was Jesus, the son of Mary; it is a true statement which they are still puzzling over. It is not God's role to adopt a son. Glory be to him! Whenever He determines upon some matter, He merely tells it: "Be!" and it is. God is my Lord and your Lord, so worship Him. This is a straight road. Factions have differed among themselves, yet how awful will it be for those who disbelieve when it comes to the spectacle on such a dreadful day! Listen to them and watch for the day when they will come to Us, though wrongdoers are in obvious error even today. Warn them of the day for regret when the matter will be decided: they act so heedlessly and still do not believe. It is We who will inherit the Earth plus anyone on it; to Us shall they return!

9.7.3   God's plea that Jews, Christians and Moslems should live in unity

3:57   Say: "People of the book, rally to a common formula to be binding on both us and you, that we shall worship only God and associate nothing else with Him, nor shall any of us take on others as lords instead of God." If they should turn away, then say: "Bear witness that we are Moslems."

It is very interesting that God's most important concern, as it is recorded in the Koran, is a simple one: One should worship only God, and associate nothing else with Him. The Holy Bible relates that, when Christ was asked which is the most important commandment of all, he said:

"The first of all the commandments is the Lord our God is one. And you shall love the Lord your God with all your heart, with all your soul, with all your mind, and with all your strength. This is the first commandment."[16]

5:5 Today wholesome things are lawful for you, and so is the food of those who were given the book lawful for you, while your food is lawful for them. And believing free women as well as free women from among those who were given the book before you, once you have given them their dowry and taken them in wedlock respectably, not seeking any thrills nor taking mistresses. Anyone who rejects faith, his action will miscarry, while he will be one who will lose out in the hereafter.

The above verse clearly underlines the commonality of Jews, Christians and Moslems by stating that marriage is allowed between these groups, and that Moslems may eat the food prepared by members of the other two groups. However, this teaching does not inhibit Moslem religious leaders from preaching its opposite. Shiite religious leaders say that intermarriage with Christians and Jews is forbidden, and that eating the meat from an animal that was killed by a Christian or Jew is forbidden.

4:130 God holds whatever is in Heaven and whatever is on Earth. We have instructed those who were given the book before you, and you as well, to heed God. If you should disbelieve, God still owns whatever is in Heaven and whatever is on Earth. God is transcendent, praiseworthy!

Even if no other verses in the Koran made known the common spiritual essence of Jews, Christians, and Moslems, the above verse leaves no doubt. It states that God instructed "those [Jews and Christians] who were given the book," as well as followers of Muhammad, to heed God. The law to heed God applies equally to all religions and is the most important of God's laws. Submitting to it would unite all of the followers of the three great religions.

9.7.4 Praise for Jews and Christians in the Koran

3:48 So God said: "Jesus, I shall gather you up and lift you towards Me, and purify you from those who disbelieve, and place those who follow you above those who disbelieve until Resurrection Day. Then to Me will be your return, and I shall decide among you concerning anything you have been disagreeing about."

The first time I read this verse in the Koran, I could hardly believe my

eyes. Even today, any Moslem I discuss this verse with is shocked. In the
Koran, God tells all Moslems that the followers of Jesus will be exalted
above the disbelievers until the Day of Resurrection.[17] While there are
some verses in the Koran that promise the world to the Moslem people if
they follow its teachings,[18] these are followed up with predictions that
they will disobey their holy book, and *not* uphold its commands. God's
prediction that the Christians will succeed in doing so is even clearer in
the following verse:

61:14   You who believe, act as God's supporters just as Jesus the son of
Mary told the disciples: "Who will be my supporters [along the way]
towards God?" The disciples said: "We are God's supporters." A faction
from the children of Israel believed, while another faction disbelieved.
We assisted the ones who believed against their enemy, till they held the
upper hand.

3:68   If you entrusted some people of the book with a large sum, they
would hand it back to you; while if you entrusted another with a gold
coin, he would never hand it back to you unless you bothered him for it
constantly. That is because they say: "There is no way for such illiterates
against us." They tell a lie about God while they realize it!

Perhaps to many it would seem specious to point out that every
human grouping contains some good and some bad, but 1400 years ago,
God must have thought it necessary to spell this out to the much simpler
societies of those times. But today, all too many Moslem religious leaders
teach their followers that all Christians and all Jews are evil people.

3:109   Yet they are not all alike: some people of the book form an upright
community; they recite God's verses through the small hours of the night
as they bow down on their knees.

4:156   And for their saying: "We killed God's messenger Christ Jesus,
the son of Mary!" They neither killed nor crucified him, even though it
seemed so to them. Those who disagree about it are in doubt concerning
it; they have no knowledge about it except by following conjecture. No
one is certain they killed him!

29:45   Do not argue with the people of the book unless it is in the
politest manner, except for those of them who do wrong. Say: "We
believe in what has been sent down to us and what has been sent down

to you. Our God and your God is [the same] One, and we are committed to [observe] peace before him."

5:85   You will find the most violently hostile people towards those who believe are the Jews and those who associate [non-believers, polytheists]; while you will find the most affectionate of them towards those who believe, are those who say: "We are Christians." That is because some of them are priests and monks; they do not behave so proudly.

While Jews were the biggest enemy of Muhammad's followers during the Prophet's lifetime, God states that the Christians, and especially the priests, were the most compassionate towards the Moslems. If God is so happy with Christians, why should we kill them and then claim that we are trying to make God happy?

7:159   Out of Moses' folk there is a nation who guided by means of the truth and dealt justly by means of it.

Moslem acquaintances of mine have called me "Jew-lover" when I told them that I did not hate Jews. Many of them believe that all Jews are evil people, and that Hitler did the world a service in killing them. My answer is to tell them that the Koran teaches us that God himself is a "Jew-lover." This verse clearly states that He is happy with all Jews who worship Him and do good. The same applies to Christians and Moslems. If it puts me in company with God, then I am proud to be called a Jew-lover—and a Christian-lover—and a Moslem-lover too.

9.7.5   The Koran's teaching that the only difference between Christians and Jews is the Christian belief in Christ as the son of God

4:169   O people of the book, do not exaggerate in your religion and tell nothing except the truth about God. Jesus Christ, the son of Mary, was merely God's messenger and His word which He cast into Mary, and a spirit from Him. Believe in God and His messengers, and do not say: "Three!" It would be better to stop. God is only one God; glory be to Him, beyond His having any son! He owns whatever is in Heaven and whatever is on Earth; God suffices as a trustee.

5:18   God thereby guides anyone who seeks His approval along pathways of peace; He leads them out of darkness into light by His permission, and guides them along a straight road. People of the book, our messenger has come to you to explain much of what you have been concealing out of the book, and to dispense with much of it. Light and a clear book have been brought to you from God.

5:19   Those who say: "God is Christ, the son of Mary," disbelieve. Say: "Who would control anything from God if He ever wanted to do away with Christ, the son of Mary and his mother, plus everyone on Earth? God holds control over Heaven and Earth, as well as anything in between them. He creates anything He wishes. God is capable of everything!"

5:21   Jews and Christians say: "We are God's children and His favorites." Say: "Then why does He punish you for your offences? Instead you are human beings just like anyone else He has created. He forgives anyone He wishes and punishes anyone He wishes. God holds control over Heaven and Earth, and whatever lies between them. Towards Him lies the goal!"

5:22   O people of the book, our messenger has come to explain to you after an interval between the messengers, lest you say: "No herald nor any warner has ever come to us." A herald and a warner has indeed come to you! God is capable of everything!

5:81   Say: "People of the book, do not exaggerate in your religion beyond the truth, nor follow the whims of a folk who have already gone astray and misled many as they stray from the level path."

In the verses above, we read warnings from God to the people of the book (Jews and Christians) that they are liable to be led from His teachings by their religious leaders. This would also be a good lesson for today's Moslems to learn.

9.7.6   The Koran's insistence that Christians should uphold the Bible and Jews the Torah

5:47-48 How can they choose you as a judge when they have the Torah, which contains God's judgment? Yet even then they will turn away, and such persons are not believers. We have sent down the Torah containing guidance and light. The prophets who were committed to [live in] peace judge those who were Jews by means of it, and [so do] the rabbis and scholars, because of what they sought to observe from God's book. They have even acted as witnesses for it. So do not dread mankind, and dread me; do not buy up my signs for a paltry price. Those who do not judge by what God has sent down are disbelievers!

Bear in mind that "what God has sent down" is not just the Koran, but the Koran, Bible, and Torah.

2:81 We gave Moses the book and followed him up with messengers later on. We gave Jesus the son of Mary evidence and assisted him with the Holy Spirit. Yet every time some messenger comes to you with what you yourselves do not like, you act uncooperatively. One group you have rejected while another group you would kill.

This verse describes how the Jews reacted historically to new prophets of God, rejecting both Jesus and Muhammad. A similar message can be seen in the New Testament.

5:50 We had Jesus, the son of Mary, follow in their footsteps in order to confirm what had come before him from the Torah and We gave him the Bible which contains guidance and Light, to confirm what He already had in the Torah [the Old Testament], and as guidance and a lesson for those who do their duty.

5:51 Let the people of the Bible judge by what God has sent down in it; those who do not judge by what God has sent down are perverts!

Here again we read that God seeks to judge each of His believers according to His book. In the case of the Christians, this is the Bible. In the case of the Jews, it is the Torah.

5:52-53 We have sent you down the book with the truth, to confirm what was already there from the previous books, and to safeguard it. Judge among them according to whatever God has sent down, and do not follow their whims concerning any truth that has been given to you. We have given each of you a code of law plus a program. If God had wished, He might have made you into one community, but compete rather in doing good deeds so He may test you by means of what He has given you. To God is your return entirely, and He will notify you concerning anything you have been disagreeing about.

5:70 If the people of the book would only believe and do their duty, we would overlook their evil deeds for them and show them into gardens full of bliss. Believing in God and doing good is always what God promises as an ingredient that will give out Heaven.

5:71   If they had only kept up the Torah and the Bible [the New Testament], and whatever was sent down to them by their Lord, they would have eaten anything above them and from beneath their feet. Some of them form a moderate community, while many of them act badly in anything they do.

The verses above teach us that if Jews, Christians and Moslems had all followed the teachings of their respective books, they would have lived in unity. However, as these messages became corrupted by man, the believers drifted apart and enmity developed between them.

5:72   Say: "People of the book, you will not make any point until you keep up the Torah and the Bible, as well as anything that has been sent down to you by your Lord." What has been sent down to you by your Lord increases many of them in arrogance and disbelief, yet do not despair about disbelieving folk.

The Koran is sent from the same source as the Torah and the Bible.

5:109-115   So God will say: "Jesus, son of Mary, remember My favor towards you and towards your mother when I assisted you with the Holy Spirit. You spoke to people from the cradle and as an adult when I taught you the book and wisdom, the Torah and the Bible. So you created something out of clay looking like a bird with My permission; you breathed into it, and by My permission it became a bird! You cured anyone born blind, and the leper with My permission. So you brought forth the dead by My permission, and I fended off the Children of Israel from you, when you brought them explanations, so those among them who disbelieved said: 'This is clearly magic!' When I inspired the disciples to believe in Me and in My messenger, they said: 'We believe, so take witness that we are Moslems.' When the disciples said: 'Jesus, son of Mary, can your Lord send a food down from Heaven for us?' he said: 'Heed God if you are believers!' They said: 'We want to eat from it, and for our hearts to feel at rest, and so we know that you have told us the truth, and that we should be witnesses for it.' Jesus the son of Mary said: 'O God our Lord, send us down a food from Heaven so it may be a recurring feast for us, for both the first of us and the last of us, and as a sign from you! Provide for us, since you are the best Provider.' [God said] I shall send it down to you. Any of you who disbelieves afterward, I shall punish with such torment as I have never punished anyone in the universe!"

In the verses above, we read the Koran's account of Jesus' last moments with his disciples—the story of the Last Supper.

61:6 So Jesus the son of Mary said: "Children of Israel, I am God's messenger to you, confirming whatever came before me in the Torah and announcing a messenger coming after me whose name will be Ahmad." Yet when he brought them explanations, they said: "This is clear magic!"

How interesting it is to see that the Koran reports that what Jesus announced to the Jews and non-believers is exactly what Muhammad announced to the Jews, Christians and non-believers centuries later. Both said that they were sent to be new prophets whose mission it was to repeat the message that God had already sent before—to cleanse the religion of the corrupt elements that had been introduced by their religious leaders in the periods between the presence of living prophets, and to urge those who still did not believe to come to God.

61:14 You who believe, act as God's supporters just as Jesus the son of Mary told the disciples: "Who will be my supporters [along the way] towards God?" The disciples said: "We are God's supporters." A faction from the children of Israel believed, while another faction disbelieved. We assisted the ones who believed against their enemy, till they held the upper hand.

In this verse, believers are referred to as those who believe in Jesus. Now, most Moslem religious leaders say that when the Koran refers to believers, it means those who followed the Prophet Muhammad. In the verse above it is made patently clear that believers consist not just of Moslems but also all of those who believe in God, including Jews and Christians.

5:116-119 When God said: "Jesus, son of Mary, have you told people: 'Take me and my mother as two gods instead of God?" he said: "Glory be to you! It is not my place to say what I have no right to. If I had said it, you would have known it already: you know what is on my mind, while I do not know anything that is on yours. You are the knower of unseen things. I have never told them anything except what you have ordered me to: Worship God as my Lord and your Lord. I was a witness for them so long as I was among them. When you gathered me up, you became the watcher over them; you are a witness for everything. If you should punish them, they are still your servants; while if you should forgive them, surely you are powerful, wise."

I find it profoundly moving to read this account in the Koran of Jesus' plea to God not to punish his followers when they claim him as God. Verse 118, above, describes Jesus as praying for his followers. In the Torah we read a similar story—that of the prophet Abraham debating with God about punishing the tribe of the Prophet Lot, saying: "God, if You find thirty good people in that tribe, will You spare them?" God agrees, and Abraham says: "What if You find twenty good people?" and God says "Yes," again. "What if You find ten good people?" Abraham wants to know, and God says once more: "Yes."[19]

28:52-4 The ones We gave the book previously believe in it. Whenever it is recited to them, they say: "We believe in it; it is the truth from our Lord! We have already committed ourselves to peace." Those will be given their payment twice over because of what they have endured; they ward off evil with good and spend some of what We have provided them with.

God recognizes that Jews and Christians are already believers. If they accept the new prophet they will be rewarded two-fold, because God realizes how difficult it will be for them to renounce the false teaching that they have lived with their whole lives.

All of the verses discussed in this section speak very clearly of a key point—the traditional trappings of Judaism and Christianity are not what God originally preached through His prophets in the Torah and the Bible. We should never forget that all three of the world's great religions are descended from the original message of Abraham:

> "Abraham was not a Jew nor a Christian but he was an upright man, a true believer [of God], and he was not one of the polytheists. Most surely the nearest of people to Abraham are those who followed him and this prophet and those who believe [in God] and God is the guardian of the believers."[20]

Although the Koran speaks out strongly against the adulteration of God's message by religious leaders through the generations, it also recognizes that ordinary believers are not responsible for the lies they are taught. God urges Moslems to discuss religion with their fellow men, with courtesy, and tells them that the Prophet Muhammad never disagreed with the Bible or the Torah.

Those Jews, Christians and Moslems who follow their faith rather than that espoused by their religious leaders, will find themselves living in harmony, as all subscribe to the simple message of belief in one God.

In the Bible, Jesus is quoted as saying that he himself is nothing, but rather that he is merely in the command of the one who sent him:

"For I came down from Heaven, not to do mine own will, but the will of Him that sent me."[21]

What can this mean but that he was only a prophet, just like the prophets before him, and that his message was no different than theirs?

Chapter 10

THE TERRORISM OF
SEPTEMBER 11TH, 2001

Shortly after the attack on America on September 11th, 2001, I had a conversation with an ardent Moslem friend who, incidentally, lives in the United States.

"The Americans have brought this upon themselves," he insisted.

Like most people around the world, I had been shocked by the attack. "How did they do that?" I asked him.

"It's because they love the Jews," he told me, in all sincerity, "They help the Jews to kill Moslems."

"Are you absolutely sure," I asked him, "that they want to help Jews kill Moslems? Don't they just have business treaties with Israel? Is that really a good reason for killing innocent Americans?"

"America is very corrupt," my friend continued, "they helped Kuwait because they wanted to make money from the oil, but they didn't help Bosnia-Herzegovina because there was no oil there to exploit."

I said, "Let's assume that they only helped Kuwait for their oil. If America chooses to help one country rather than another, does that justify taking the lives of ordinary Americans? Does the Koran preach that?"

"No," he admitted, "but look at the CIA. They're so corrupt. They help people like the Shah of Iran because he gave them whatever they wanted. They helped Saddam Hussein fight against Iran, and then they kicked him out of Kuwait after making him what he was. They promoted the war between Iran and Iraq so that they could sell their weapons."

I told him, "In the Koran it says that one should always be completely sure before saying anything.[1] Everything you've said should be backed up by complete documentary evidence. But let's assume for the sake of argument that you have evidence of America selling weapons to Iraq and not to Iran. If the United States decides to sell to one country and not another, that is within their rights. For the Iranian government to say that the United States is the 'Great Satan', and that it would rather buy its weapons on the black market (which gets its weapons from America anyway), so as to make the Iranian people believe it doesn't trade with America, is a much greater sin. For the American government to sell is not an act of ungodliness—it's a business. For example, we cannot punish a gun shop owner for killing if the person who buys a gun from him commits a murder.

"But even if America has done all the bad things you say, let's count all the good things it has done, from promoting world peace to funding education. Let's look at how the American government has used its people's taxes by maintaining the country well, by providing a good educational system, by creating plenty of jobs and a level of freedom whereby anyone can achieve anything. Doesn't all of this counter the suspicions you have about America? Imagine if Iran was doing the same. Would it be a good country, according to your standards? Do you hate America just because it is America? Has Iran ever accomplished more for its people, even in the days of the Persian Empire? Isn't it true that this young country has a lot to teach ancient civilizations? In just a few centuries, long-established cultures have learned to respect America for all it has achieved.

"There are corrupt people in every government—one can only judge them by their results. America has a lot to offer to its people, more than any country has ever offered in the past. For that, many countries are jealous and cannot see all the good it does. This is especially true of those people who are taught to hate America from babyhood. Religious leaders become popular among their people when they put America down. Khomeni knew this, and he used this knowledge by saying: 'America is the Great Satan.' When he said that, his popularity soared. The popular chant 'Death to America' brought Khomeni more power than any man had ever held in Iran. Arab religious leaders are learning that if one cannot set up a good system, it suffices to speak out against America to make your people love you. This kind of ideology in the hands of fanatical Moslems will do wonders for the devil, who is proud of them. I don't believe that he himself could do a better job than the men who massacred innocent people on September 11th, 2001. The devil knew that there would be men who were prepared to take his side—but I don't think he ever imagined that they would be men who would, for his sake, die with

God's name on their lips.

"Instead of thoughtfulness, Moslem religious leaders instilled fanaticism in their people. The more they pray, the more ignorant they become. It's as if God is not listening. But He is! The Moslem fanatics are not saying the right things, and clearly they are not doing the right things. Massacres of Palestinians by Israelis are wrong. Killing Israelis on the part of Palestinians is also wrong. Killing Americans is wrong too. Killing as a way of avoiding facing the task of working in a godly way is always wrong. In the Koran, God has permitted people to kill only in self defense. The Koran has never said that one can kill people because they come from a successful country that promotes the accumulation of knowledge."

My friend remained unconvinced.

Will the terrorists who committed the attacks against the great nation that is America go to Heaven because they thought they were doing the work of God? The Koran says that when people die, and justify their actions by saying, "…but we were following those who went before," will be punished for having knowledge of God's law but not following it.[2]

God gave human beings the gifts of intelligence and free will. If we ignore these gifts and choose instead to do what others tell us, we will live in ignorance until the day we die. This is the way the instigators of those terrible acts must have lived. They believed that they were doing the work of God. As they approached their gates, they must have wondered if they were doing the right thing. In all cases of fanaticism, there are those who ignore the pleas of their conscience, and instead do the devil's work. Some even shout, "God is the greatest," before they kill His creations.

Religious contamination of the conscience is always behind such acts. But how does it occur? Imagine the life of a woman who is a heavily dependent drug user. When she gets pregnant, and gives birth to a little girl, the child is also an addict. Her mother injects her with heroin to stop her cries, and the child becomes unable to avoid being addicted. As she becomes older, she drifts into prostitution and petty crime to support her habit. Almost every man she meets abuses her, and there is never a reason to stop taking drugs. She has no belief in God's mercy, because she has never known what it is to be loved. The devil is much more familiar to her! Little by little, her inborn conscience deteriorates until she is as abusive as her abusers. This is the heritage of her mother. An innocent little girl has become a bad person, and a chain reaction is set in place. When she becomes a mother in turn, she will bring up her child the only way she knows how—and so on through the generations.

When God told Adam's son who killed his brother, that when one person kills another, he will be punished for destroying a whole generation, He was referring to exactly this sort of chain reaction. Those who set these sequences of evil behavior in place will be punished greatly, while God will acknowledge those who contribute more to life than life gave them.

The Koran and the Bible both say that the more given, the more required.[3] Those who have been blessed with an easy life find it easy to live in peace. But those for whom life seems to be a series of cruel injustices wonder why God has given them so little, while He has given others so much more. It is important for everyone to understand that if they live well, regardless of their circumstances on Earth, they will be rewarded. Perhaps every second of misery throughout the course of a long, tragic life will be repaid by a thousand lifetimes of happiness!

What does all of this have to do with suicide bombers? Well, although these are adults, they are not unlike the drug-addict's baby. They have been brainwashed throughout their whole lives, and have never had the chance to learn about the true nature of God. They will be judged—but they will be judged much less harshly than those who taught them and led them to commit these evil deeds. However evil they may be, they are nothing when compared with their instructors, who knowingly and willingly performed the devil's work and reduced their students to the status of animals, by keeping them in a state of profound ignorance. True learning comes from exercising the mind and questioning oneself. In organized religion, this option is never available. Members of the public are told that they must not question the ways of the past, and that they should accept everything they are told if they want to demonstrate their faith in God. Once this lesson has been taught, it is easy to encourage them to commit murder in the name of God. Those who become so indoctrinated are now able to resist the voice of their conscience and the sense of humanity that is their birthright. Of course, there are always those who do listen to their own hearts and do the right thing. In any war or conflict, the hardest death to inflict is the first. Any soldier will tell you that. But only killing in a rare, just situation is allowed, and only this allows the killer to live with a clear conscience. The Koran instructs us in no uncertain terms that we may only kill in self-defense.[4]

Our consciences are gifts from God. They never lie. Only those who have been rigorously trained to ignore the voice of their conscience can commit evil acts—just like the Catholic priests who abuse innocent children and still find ways of justifying their deeds, as well as their religious superiors who do not hesitate to hide what they have done. All of these are doing the devil's work.

True Judaism, Christianity and Islam are beautiful, preaching love of God and of humanity. But these religions are corrupted by the devil's agents. Today, more than ever, we need to be very aware of this.

The attack of September 11th was the work of the devil. It is my belief that the majority of the hijackers were unaware that the planes they seized control of were intended to crash and kill all on board. I believe that the pilots alone were cognizant of the evil goals of their mission. They would not have risked the possibility that some of their men would have a last moment change of heart. They knew how hard it would be for them to see the women and children on the plane and still continue with the evil plan. To some extent, they too were victims in these atrocious acts of genocide because they will receive hell when they were led to believe the opposite. Lives which could have been given to serving God were wasted in the service of the devil.

Chapter 11

OVERLOOKED MESSAGES OF THE KORAN

Most Moslems obtain their understanding of the Koran from the interpretations of their religious leaders. Few ever question what they are told to believe. But the holy book contains many messages that might shock them from their complacency. For example, in the Koran there is a verse saying:

"God said to Jesus: I shall gather you up and lift you toward me, and purify you from those who disbelieve, and place those who follow you above those who disbelieve until the Resurrection Day."[1]

The above verse says very simply that Christians will be above the non-believers until the resurrection. Moreover, the Koran states:

"Do not falter and feel saddened since you are superior, if you are believers."[2]

The most reasonable conclusion to this is that among all believers, whether they are Jews, Christians, or Moslems, only one group will be above the non-believers and only one group will be superior. That group will be comprised of the believers who are the followers of Jesus (Christians). However, had Jews or Moslems been true believers, living according to the word of God, they would have been superior. Their failure to accomplish this is clearly seen today as the Jews' massacre of innocent Moslems disqualifies them as true believers and the fanaticism of Moslems disqualifies them even as civilized people, let alone superior believers. As America's power is not even matched by the rest of the world put together, the power of the Koran is clearly seen in its prediction of this fact.

According to Shiite religious leaders, if a Moslem touches a Jew or Christian with a wet hand, he must purify himself by washing that part of the body three times, as Jews and Christians are impure (similar types of

purification ritual must be observed when one touches a dog). How can
this be, when the Koran invariably discusses Christians with the utmost
respect, saying:

> "They [Christians and Jews] are not all alike; of the followers
> of the book there is an upright party; they recite God's communi-
> cations in the night time and they adore [God]. They believe in
> God and the last day, and they enjoin what is right and forbid the
> wrong, and they strive with one another in hastening to good
> deeds, and those are among the good. And whatever good they
> do, they shall not be denied it, and God knows those who guard
> [against evil]."[3]

Surely the religious leaders have something other than God on their
minds when they write their rules.

Many people have been prompted in recent days to ask just why so
many Moslems despise the United States. The main reason is because of
their respect for the religious leaders that guide them. Most Moslems
have not received the benefits of a high standard of education, and they
look with awe at the most educated person in their midst—usually the
religious leader. They never even try to question his dictates. When religious leaders seek to bolster their popularity, they set themselves against
a mighty adversary—and what enemy is more powerful than the United
States? But that's not all. Being men, they also don't hesitate to pit themselves against the weaker members of a deeply misogynist society—the
women, who are usually even less educated than the men. The opinions
religious leaders hold about women are truly shocking. One of the most
respected Shiite religious leaders stated in his book that women are a type
of animal—they aren't even human.[4] God decided to give them human
faces so that men would not be too disgusted to talk to them, and would
be able to bring themselves to mate with them.

> Mullah Sadrah, one of the greatest philosophers of the
> Moslem era, has said a very disturbing thing about women being
> animals, and referred to them as animals which are good for mat-
> ing, and the late Mullah Hadi Sabzavari has taken this and
> expanded on it, saying that it's true. Women are not that different
> from the poor animals. God put human faces on these animals so
> that men would not be disgusted when conversing with them,
> and would approach them for mating. These are the words of a
> philosopher ...[5]

With the exception of this great writer, no one has ever voiced disagreement.

Moslems are not born with a greater propensity to hatred than anybody else. They learn to hate, and their instructors are the religious leaders of Islam. Just as computers produce nonsense if they are programmed with nonsense, so do humans produce hatred if they are fed hatred.

Chapter 12

GOD'S LAWS IN THE KORAN VS. THE LAWS CREATED BY MAN

Of the three major religions which dominate the world stage today—Islam, Judaism and Christianity—Islam is the only one based upon a book which remains true to its original content (the Torah and the Bible have undergone many changes over time, resulting in many different translations). Even with the consistency of the Koran, there is little or no unity among the followers of Islam. The lifestyle and system of belief of the Shiites is largely based upon the teachings of religious leaders, whose mindsets and belief systems are formed in religious institutions designed for this purpose. The highest religious position attainable is that of ayatollah. When one reaches this position, one usually writes a rule book (again, this is known as a *resalah*). These rule books are the root of the problems facing Shiite Moslems today. While the Sunni do not have a rule book, they are subject to similar supreme religious leaders. However, their lives are somewhat less dictated by the authorities. I was raised as a Shiite Moslem, and my greater familiarity with this group leads me to focus on it in this book.

The rules which, together, make up the *resalah* have been passed from ayatollah to ayatollah since the beginning of the religious hierarchies in Islam. *Resalahs* have been an integral part of the Shiite Moslem faith during the last 450 years, during which time no ayatollah has ever questioned a single one of the man-made rules they contain, regardless of the considerable extent to which they contradict the laws of the Koran.

The man-made laws I quote are taken mostly from the writings of the most famous Shiite ayatollah, Mousavie Khomeni, and the texts from the

Koran are taken directly from the source. While Shiite Moslems can choose whichever religious leader they prefer, all are obliged to blindly follow the religious rules they are told, rules which vary little from one religious leader to the next.

All supreme religious leaders have a *resalah* which they teach to their followers. The rules contained in this book, and not the teachings of the Koran, are what guide these Moslems through life, determining both their spiritual and their secular choices. If, in the course of daily living, they encounter a problem that is not covered by the *resalah*, they must go to their religious leader and ask him what to do. A shocking fact is that Shiite Moslems have a provision that allows them to do whatever they want, simply by asking the Koran how they should do it. In other words, if one of them takes it into his mind to blow up a building in the name of God, he can pray: "God, please show me whether or not I should blow up the building" and then open the Koran. Religious leaders have written "bad" and "good" in the right upper corner of the various pages and, according to what the follower reads, he interprets the answer. If the page says "good" he supposes that God wants him to blow up the building, if "bad" that He does not. Regardless of the importance or lack of importance attached to any issue, Shiite faithful are encouraged to consult the Koran for guidance in this manner. I remember my Mom carefully consulting the Koran for guidance—but if the book "told" her that she should not do something she really wanted to do, she would reword the question slightly and ask again until she got the answer that she was looking for. Of course, she would be happy then, because she was sure that she was doing God's will!

Before presenting the evidence, it cannot be reiterated strongly enough that the laws of the *resalah* bear no resemblance to those in the Koran. In the past, when I made this point to deeply fanatic Moslems, they've always laughed and insisted that I should stop reading the Koran. The most widely accepted interpretation of the Koran is that of Ayatollah Tabatabaie, who is one of the most respected of the leaders of the Shiite Moslems. In his introduction to the interpretation, he has written:

"The Koran introduces itself as the most clear light for guidance. So how could anyone claim that they are going to explain the Koran so the word of God can be clear?"[1]

Tabatabaie stresses repeatedly that the word of God is easy to comprehend, stating that the knowledge that the Koran embodies is like a great light, and he who tries to improve it is like a man trying to illuminate the sun with a flashlight. He further states that the Koran is best understood by someone without prejudice—someone unencumbered by the false truths he thinks he already knows. He says that whoever reads the Koran with hatred in his heart will find no trouble in interpreting its message to confirm the unholy desires he already feels. To understand the Koran, Tabatabaie reiterates, one does not need to be a scholar, a genius or a religious leader. He says that to whoever reads this great book, God reveals the secret of understanding it, just as He does in the Bible and in the Torah, and that God's book leaves no room for doubt.

"This book, there is no doubt in it, is a guide to those who guard [against evil]."[2]

Tabatabaie also says that the Koran is very easy for good-hearted people to understand. He adds that in the Koran it says of those who have sickness in their hearts, that God will multiply their sickness, and they still think they understand.[3] (This passage of the Koran explains how terrorists justify their actions in the name of God.)

However, in spite of all the beautiful words written by Tabatabaie, he himself did not live or teach according to them, nor did the religious leaders who so revered him. In fact, Tabatabaie never spoke against the ungodly laws of the *resalahs*, but instead chose to live according to them. His hypocrisy is overwhelming.

Not long before the tragedy that occurred on American soil on September 11th, 2001, I visited a mosque near my home, to which I had been invited by my Moslem friends to give a speech. They knew that I had been researching the Koran for some time, and were interested to hear what I had discovered. I gave two talks there, and after the second, I was asked not to return and speak of such things again. Some members of the congregation even became angry and accused me of being a member of a defamatory organization sent to spy on them in the mosque—one even threatened to "teach me the Koran with his fist."

This sort of reaction is common among Moslems, and I can understand it. As a very young man, I was an ardent follower of Ayatollah Khomeni, and even returned to Iran to fight with his troops against Iraq. Although my views have changed radically, I can't blame myself for my former fanaticism. I wanted to make my people happy. They told me to believe in God, and I did. They told me to pray according to the laws of the *resalah*, and I did. They told me to live according to the rules of the *resalah*, and I did that, too. I was prepared to do anything that would make God happy. An earnest wish to please God is a beautiful thing, but God's words can be hidden from people by their religious leaders.

But Moslems are not prone to violence or slavishly following violent men more than other people. The behavior of certain Moslems today is matched by that of European Christians in the Middle Ages when they launched their blood-thirsty "crusade" against the Arab people of the Middle East. They believed that they were justified in slaughtering, raping and destroying Arab people in the name of Christianity, much as Islamic terrorists justify their actions today.

Remember, most Moslems, believing themselves to be devout, are not aware that the dictates of the ayatollahs they follow are not also the dictates of the Koran. Shiite Moslems choose the ayatollah they esteem most highly, and then follow his rules. Religious leaders have managed to convince their followers that they are dependent on them for salvation. This book exposes the falsity of this notion, as it systematically compares the dictates of the rule books with the original teachings of the Koran.

Shiite Moslem Doctrine (resalah)

Rules 1 to **14** are laws pertaining to the obedience of supreme religious authorities.

For example, in **rule 1** it states that a Moslem must accept the principal laws of Islam as reasonable and logical. However, they must follow the other laws under the guidance of a supreme religious authority who understands the reasoning behind them.

This law, if it is followed, ensures that Moslem people will not think for themselves, but will simply do what their religious leaders tell them.

Exact words of the Koran

45:5 These are the verses of God's book, to whom besides God's verses and words will you turn?

21:10 We have sent down a book to you, which contains your reminder. Will you not use your reason?

6:115 Your Lord's word has been completed so far as [its] credibility and justice are concerned; there is no way to change His words. He is the alert, the aware.

18:26 Quote whatever has been revealed to you from your Lord's book: no one is allowed to change His words, nor will you ever find any sanctuary except in Him. So read what is sent to you in this book, which is from your God, no one is allowed to substitute these words.

In the *resalah* religious leaders say that there are rules that are not in the Koran and that Moslems need them to learn the laws that were omitted. The following verses from the Koran prove this wrong:

7:1-2   A book has been sent down to you, so do not let your chest feel it is under any constraint because of it, so you may warn by means of it; a reminder for believers. Follow whatever has been sent down to you by your Lord and do not follow any sponsors besides Him; yet how seldom do you remember!

7:50   We have given them the book; We have spelled it out knowingly as a guideline and mercy for folk who believe.

10:64   [You] will have good news concerning worldly life as well as the hereafter. There is no way to alter God's words; that will be the supreme achievement.

11:1-2   ... [This is] a book whose verses are decisive, and have been set forth in detail in the presence of someone [who is] wise, informed, that you will serve only God [alone]: "I am a warner, a herald from Him to you."

18:1-3   Praise be to God, who has sent down the book for His servants and has placed no distortion in it, [it is] straightforward, so He may warn about serious violence from Himself and give good news to believers who perform honorable deeds. They will have a handsome wage, to bask in forever and ever.

18:26-27   Quote whatever has been revealed to you from your Lord's book: there is no one who may change His words, nor will you ever find any sanctuary except in Him. Restrain yourself concerning those who appeal to their Lord in the morning and evening, wanting His presence; yet do not let your eyes wander too far from them, desiring the attraction of worldly life. Do not obey anyone whose heart We allow to neglect remembering Us, so he pursues his own whim. He will become dissipated.

44:3   In it [the Koran] every wise matter is set forth.

45:19   These are insights for mankind, as well as guidance and mercy for folk who are convinced.

45:24   Whenever Our clear verses are recited to them, their argument is merely to say: "Bring back our forefathers if you are so truthful."

45:58   We have made it easy for your tongue [to recite] in order that they may bear this in mind.

39:29   An Arabic Koran possessing no ambiguity so that they may do their duty.

39:42 We have sent you down the book with truth for mankind ...

27:1 These are verses from the Koran which is a clear book to understand.

26:1 These are verses from the book which is very clear.

19:97 We have made it easy for your tongue so you may announce good news about it to those who do their duty, and warn headstrong folk by means of it.

14:1 We have sent down a book to you in order to bring men out of darkness into light by their Lord's permission, towards the road of the powerful, the praiseworthy.

There are at least 155 more verses in the Koran confirming that the book was sent from God for the benefit of humankind without need of change or interpretation.[4]

Shiite Moslem Doctrine (resalah)

Rules 15 to **71** cover the laws of cleanliness. For example, **rules 15** and **16** state that there are five kinds of water, one of which is called "kor water." This is the kind of water that, if poured into a pan, fills it when its width, length and depth are three and a half times the width of an open hand. As experts differ as to the details of this rule, we must assume that, in general, water is kor if it weighs 377 kilos divided by 419 kilos. **Rule 65** discusses the three instances in which the anus must only be cleaned with water: when, together with the natural waste that is excreted, unclean matter such as blood appears; when something unclean from outside the body comes in contact with the anus; when the area around the anus is more dirty than usual. When none of these circumstances occur, the anus can be cleaned with water, a cloth or a stone. However, washing with water is preferable.

Exact words of the Koran

In the Koran, as in the Bible, the term "cleanliness" is usually used to refer to cleanliness of the heart, and not the body. However, there are a few references to personal hygiene.

8:11 ... and send down water from the sky on you to cleanse you...

9:109 ... God loves those who cleanse themselves...

Shiite Moslems are so fanatical about the rituals of cleanliness that they spend hours a day ensuring that they follow them. But still, when one goes to an Iranian mosque to pray, the filthiness of the bathrooms is overwhelming, as is the strong smell of unclean bodies. More attention is paid to ritual than hygiene.

Shiite Moslem Doctrine (resalah)	Exact words of the Koran
Rules 72 to **77** cover the laws that govern the cleaning of one's penis after urinating. For example, **rule 72**, known as the "Mosta-hab" or that which is better to do, covers the rituals that men must perform after urinating. The rule can be followed in many different ways, the best method being described as follows: once the man has finished urinating, if his anus has become impure, he should purify by following three steps. Firstly, he must pull the middle finger of the left hand from the anus to the root of the penis, three times; secondly, he must place his thumb on the penis, and the adjacent finger under the penis, and pull three times until he reaches the circumcision mark; thirdly, he must push the head of the penis three times.	Nothing in the Koran corresponds to these laws.

Moslem religious leaders seem to believe that God is so concerned about a few drops of left-over urine that He expects a man to spend hours of his time following the above rules. Obviously, there is no mention of this sort of thing in the Koran.

Shiite Moslem Doctrine (resalah)	Exact words of the Koran
Rules 78 to **82** are known as "Mak-rohat," which means "things that are not forbidden but it is better not to do" and "Mos-tahabat," or "things that are recommended but not commanded to do." For example, **rule 78** states that it is preferable to urinate or defecate where no one can see you, and that one should put the left foot first on entering the bathroom and exit right foot first. While sitting on the toilet, it is preferable to cover your head and put your weight on your left foot.	Nothing in the Koran corresponds to these laws.
Rule 82 recommends that one urinate before praying to God or sleeping and both before and after having sex.	
Rule 83 defines that which is "najest" or impure as comprising the following eleven things: Human urine. Human body waste. Sperm. A dead animal that is not killed according to the rule book. Blood. Dogs. Pigs. Atheists. Intoxicating drink. Beer. Sweat from a camel that has eaten any of the above.	Nothing in the Koran corresponds to these laws.

(I wonder how many camels are in the habit of consuming intoxicating liquor, and if they're willing to confess it when they do!)

Shiite Moslem Doctrine (resalah)	Exact words of the Koran
Rules 84 to **120** expand upon **rule 83**. For example, **rule 119** states that if one attains orgasm from a sinful source, and then has sexual contact with one's lawful partner, one should avoid one's own sweat and clean it off before praying. However, if one has sexual contact with a lawful partner and then has orgasm from a sinful source, one can pray with sweat still on the body.	Nothing in the Koran corresponds to these laws.
Rules 121 to **124** cover the ways in which one can determine whether something is najest—impure. For example, **rule 122** states that if a dish or cloth is unclean, you must assume that it has not been cleaned. If you doubt that a clean dish or cloth has become unclean, then you should assume that it is clean.	Nothing in the Koran corresponds to these laws.
Rules 125 to **134** describe the ways in which clean things can become impure. These include the impurity that results when an unclean object touches a clean object, if one of them was damp in such a way that the dampness could travel from one to another. However, if the amount of dampness is so small that it does not pass from one object to another, its cleanliness is not affected.	Nothing in the Koran corresponds to these laws.

These laws have made the lives of many Moslems a misery. The fearful uneducated feel that if they fail to wash themselves in complete accordance with God's will, He will be unhappy with them. Seeing this, the comment that God makes in the Bible when He spoke to the religious leaders saying, "You will make harsh rules for the people to follow, but will do nothing about them yourself," rings very true.[5]

There are millions of examples of people suffering because of these laws. For instance, my mother's cousin is so obsessive that when she washes her hands, she often does so for fifteen minutes to make sure that she is following the rules of the religious leaders properly. Recently, she had her house painted. One of the painters had cut his finger, and was bleeding slightly, so he put a bandage on the wound. When he had finished painting, someone told her about the bleeding finger, and she told her husband that she would never pray in their house because blood, which is impure, had gotten into the paint.

When I was a university student I roomed with a number of very fanatical Moslems. One of them would always carry a handkerchief with him so that when he had to open a door, he could take it out and use it so as not to have to touch the handle. He would never use the bathroom, choosing instead to wait until he got home. These restrictions caused him so much difficulty that they began to affect his studies.

Other friends of mine were worried on the days when it rained that a Christian acquaintance might touch their hands or even tap them on the shoulder. Instead of concentrating on their studies, they exerted all their mental efforts in prayer to God and in avoiding breaking the many complex rules.

Once a Moslem clergyman came to the campus to speak to the Moslem students. After the speech, some of the students asked him whether the washer-dryers in the dormitories were najest (impure), or if they could be used. He answered that they were impure because they were used by Christians. All the Moslem students were then obliged to wash all their clothes by hand and dry them from lines hung in their rooms! Less fanatical students would use the washer and not the dryer. About a year later, we visited the Berkley campus to hear another clergyman. More than 400 attended, and after the speech, a student asked, "Can we dry our clothes in the American dryers?"

"Of course," came the reply, "why not?"

The student answered by saying, "The wet clothes would touch the inside of the dryer, which had previously been in contact with the wet clothes of Christians, making it dirty, and another clergyman told us that this is unacceptable."

The clergyman's answer was, "I am a follower of Ayatollah Monteseri and he said that when you place wet clothes in the machine after the cycle has been finished, the water does not pass through the clothes, leaving them damp but not wet. For this reason it is permissible to use a washing machine after a Christian." All the students that had previously avoided using dryers were delighted that their lives would become easier again.

In the Koran, a message that is often repeated is that the holy book was written so as to make life easier for everybody![6]

Shiite Moslem Doctrine (resalah)	Exact words of the Koran
Rules 135 to **147** are the laws of "Ne-ja-saat," or impure things. For example, **rule 147** states that even if a child who is old enough to know right from wrong—perhaps a child close to puberty—says that he has washed an object, you must wash it again anyway. However, if this person states that the object they are holding is unclean, this should be accepted.	Nothing in the Koran corresponds to these rules.
Rules 148 to **224** cover the issue of cleanliness and how to become clean. For example, **rule 161** refers to an infant boy who is still nursing, has not yet eaten solid food and has never drunk pig's milk. If his urine comes in contact with anything, that object is unclean. However, it can be cleaned by pouring water on it in such a way that the water touches all parts that came in contact with his urine. It is recommended that water be poured on the object one more time. However, if the object is of the nature of clothing or carpet, it does not need to be rinsed.	Nothing in the Koran corresponds to these rules.

Shiite Moslem Doctrine (resalah)

Rules 225 to **235** are the laws of dishes and how they should be treated. For example, **rule 232** states that one can take food from a gold or silver dish and place it in another dish. However, it is forbidden to do so if the food was changed from one dish to another because one is not allowed to eat from gold or silver.

Rules 236 to **344** are the laws covering the issue of washing before praying. For example, **rule 237** states that one must wash the length of the face from the top of forehead—the hairline—to the end of the chin, and the width of the face from the point where the thumb and the middle finger can reach. If even a little of this area is left unwashed, then the washing is not accepted. To be certain that one has washed all these areas, one should also wash beyond them.

Exact words of the Koran

Nothing in the Koran corresponds to these rules. However, in the Bible, Christ refers to religious leaders who teach and clean dishes with care, but forget to cleanse the heart.[7]

5:8 You who believe, whenever you intend to pray, wash your faces and your hands up to the elbows, and wipe off your heads and your feet up to the ankle.

Sunni Moslems, like Shiites, wash before they pray to God. In the Koran, it says that one should wash the hands to the elbow, wash the face and brush the feet and hair clean. The Shiite wash from hand to elbow, the Sunni from the elbow to the hand. Even this is cause for discussion. It's not always easy to follow the rules for washing—public washrooms are not the easiest places for taking off shoes and socks and washing the feet.

God does say in the Koran that He wants us to be clean for prayer. However, the Koran was sent to people who lived in the desert, at a time when the Arabs, who had little opportunity to bathe, lived in very unhygienic circumstances. But today, in the twenty first century, most people have all the resources necessary for proper hygiene.

Shiite Moslem Doctrine (resalah)

Rules 345 to **391** are the laws concerning the exit of sperm from the body and how to clean afterwards. For example, **rule 349** says that if a man has intercourse, and inserts his penis to the depth of the circumcision mark or more, whether into a man or a woman, and whether into the front or the back, with a child or an adult, then one is considered "Jo-nab" (in a situation calling for the washing of the whole body) whether orgasm is reached or not. **Rule 351** states that if one has sex with an animal—sexual contact to the point of reaching orgasm—washing the whole body is enough. If one does not reach orgasm, one should still wash the whole body, even if it had recently been washed before prayer. If one engages in sex with an animal without having washed before prayer, it is strongly recommended that one wash the whole body and also perform the washing ceremony for prayer. **Rule 353** says that if one cannot wash the whole body, one can perform "Ta-Ya-Mom" (a procedure that should be carried out when water is not available). If one has sex for no good reason when the time comes to pray, this is a problem. However, if the sex was motivated by either joy or fear for one's safety, there is no problem. **Rule 348** says that one should urinate after reaching orgasm. However, if one does not urinate, and finds that liquid exits from the penis after washing, this liquid must be considered to be sperm, and the whole body must be washed again.

Exact words of the Koran

Nothing in the Koran corresponds to these rules.

Without a doubt, anyone with a degree of reason would be absolutely horrified on reading these rules.

The Koran says: "After being with your wife, clean yourself." The religious leaders interpret this as meaning, "You must immerse yourself totally in water three times." This rule causes immense hardship to people who live in countries with regular drought. Remember that God spoke to Muhammad who preached to people who lived very simple lives in the desert. Today, telling a civilized person that one should wash after intercourse is truly offensive.

Shiite Moslem Doctrine (resalah)	Exact words of the Koran
Rules 392 to **520** are the laws about women's menstruation. For example, **rule 404** states that if a woman does not know which category applies to her (i.e. she is bleeding, but it is not her regular period), when she wants to pray she should take some cotton and place it in her vagina and then take it out. Judging by the amount of blood on the cotton, she should decide whether her bleeding is strong, medium or weak, and then do that which is prescribed under that category. But if she knows that the type of bleeding she has is constant, then before prayer she must perform the acts covered by the relevant law.	**2:222** They will ask you about menstruation. Say: "It is a nuisance, so keep away from women during menstruation." Do not approach them until they are cleansed. Once they cleanse themselves, then go to them just as God has commanded you to do. God loves the penitent and he loves those who try to keep clean.
Rule 470 states that if a woman enters the prayer time, and knows that her period will arrive if she waits to pray, she should pray immediately.	Nothing in the Koran corresponds to these rules.
Rules 521 to **540** are the laws referring to how a person who has been in contact with a dead body should wash. For example, **rule 523** states that if one's hair touches a dead body, or one's body touches the hair of a dead person, washing the whole body is recommended.	Nothing in the Koran corresponds to these rules.

Shiite Moslem Doctrine (resalah)	Exact words of the Koran
Rules 541 to **637** are the laws of how to treat the dead before burying, how they should be buried, and how to perform the funeral before burial. For example, **rule 555** states that the person who washes the cadaver before the burial must be a Moslem and a believer in the twelve apostles of Muhammad. He must be wise, over the age of puberty, and familiar with all the religious laws concerning washing the whole body.	Nothing in the Koran corresponds to these rules.
Rules 638 to **640** refer to the prayers that Moslems should perform when they are afraid.	In the Koran it says: "Fear nobody but God."[8]
Rules 641 to **643** refer to the laws of digging up a dead body.	Nothing in the Koran corresponds to these rules.
Rules 644 to **647** deal with recommended baptisms, or washing of the entire body. There are many such occasions in Islam—Fridays, days of fasting, etc. For example, **rule 644** states that the baptism of the month of fasting occurs on the first day of the month, and on all odd days thereafter until the 21st of the month., Baptism is recommended every night from the 21st on, and also on the special days of the 15th, 17th, 19th, 21st, 23rd, 27th and 28th. Baptism can be undertaken at any time during the night, although the best time is close to sunset. After the 21st day of the month, baptism should occur between the "Maghreb" and "Esha" prayers.	Nothing in the Koran corresponds to these rules.

Shiite Moslem Doctrine (resalah)

Rules 648 to **727** cover everything that should be done to prepare for prayer if there is no water. For example, **rule 648** says that if one is in a valley, one should seek water to wash before praying until exhausting all the possibilities, but if one is in the middle of nowhere—and especially if the land is hilly or if there are trees which make it hard to search—then one should search in four directions, to a distance equivalent to that traveled by an arrow shot from a bow. However, if the land is not as described, one should look twice as far. **Rule 649** states that if, in accordance with **rule 648**, one searches in four directions, but some directions are flat and others not, then one should search the flat land for twice the distance than when one is in hilly land. This distance has been described as equivalent to 200 walking steps.

Exact words of the Koran

4:46 You who believe, do not attempt to pray while you are drunk, until you know what you are saying. Nor after a seminal emission, except when traveling along some road—until you wash. If you are ill or on a journey, or one of you has come from the toilet, or has had contact with women and you have not found any water, then pick up some wholesome soil and wipe your faces and your hands with it. God is pardoning and forgiving.

5:8-9 You who believe, whenever you intend to pray, wash your faces and your hands up to the elbows, and wipe off your heads and your feet up to the ankle. If you are ritually soiled, then wash. If you are ill or are on a journey, or one of you has just come from the toilet or had contact with any women and you do not find any water then resort to wholesome soil and use it to wipe your faces and hands. God does not want to place any inconvenience on you, but he does want to purify you and complete his favor for you in order that you may act thankfully.

Shiite Moslem Doctrine (resalah)

Rules 729 to **774** refer to the times for prayer and the laws governing them. For example, **rule 757** says that if one realizes with certainty that one has not performed the noon prayer while performing the afternoon prayer, one should consider the afternoon prayer to be the noon one, and the afternoon prayer must be repeated. However, if one is mistaken, and realizes that the original assumption of performing the afternoon prayer was correct, one must redo all parts of the prayer as is proper. Then the prayer is accepted.

Exact words of the Koran

4:104 ...prayer is a timely prescription for believers.

7:204 Keep your Lord in mind within your own soul, beseeching and fearfully, without raising your voice, both in the early morning and in evening, do not act so unaware.

11:116 Keep up prayer at both ends of the day and at the approach of the night. Good deeds remove evil deeds. That is a reminder for such persons as will be reminded.

17:80 Keep up prayer from the decline of the sun, until twilight at night; and [observe] the reading at daybreak, since reading [the Koran] at daybreak will be witnessed.

17:110 Say: "Appeal to God, or appeal to the mercy-giving: whichever [name] you may invoke, he still has the finest names. Do not shout in your prayer nor say it under your breath; seek a course in between."

20:130 So be patient about anything they may say and hymn your Lord's praise before the sun's rise and before its setting, and in the small hours of the night. Hymn it as well at the ends of the day so that you may meet approval.

Shiite Moslem Doctrine (resalah)

Rules 776 to **787** determine the direction that should be faced while praying. For example, **rule 784** states that if one has no tools to assist in finding the direction of Mecca and if, despite trying, it proves impossible to identify the direction, then one must perform the prayer four times, in four directions. If there is no time to pray four times, then one must pray as much as time allows. If there is only time to pray once, one can pray in any direction, and perform all the prayers in the knowledge that at least one was in the right direction. If there is deviation from the proper direction, it should not be more than all the way to the right and all the way to the left.

Exact words of the Koran

2:109 The east and west are God's: wherever you may turn, there will be God's countenance, for God is boundless, aware.

2:119 Thus we set up the house as are [made] for mankind and as a sanctuary, and [said]: "Adopt Abraham's station as a place for prayer." We entrusted Abraham and Ishmael with cleaning out My house for those who circle around it and are [praying] there, and who bow down on their knees in worship.

2:172 Virtue does not mean for you to turn your faces towards the east and west, but virtue means one should believe in God [alone], the last day, angels, the book and prophets; and no matter how he loves it, to give his wealth away to near relatives, orphans, the needy, the wayfarer and beggars, and towards freeing captives; and to keep up prayer and pay the welfare tax; and those who keep their word whenever they promise anything; and are patient under suffering and hardship and in times of violence. Those are the ones who act loyally, and they perform their duty.

Shiite Moslem Doctrine (resalah)

Rules 788 to **865** refer to covering one's body and observing laws concerning it while praying. For example, **rule 800** states that God does not accept a prayer if one's body or clothes are unclean. A lack of awareness of the law does not mean that the prayers are accepted. **Rule 807** says that if anyone is unsure as to the cleanliness of their clothes or body and prays to God, but later realizes that they were unclean, their prayers will not be accepted.

Rules 866 to **899** refer to the laws governing the places to pray. **Rule 888** says that, if a man and woman are separated by a wall or curtain or something else, their prayer is correct and they do not need to pray again.

Rules 900 to **915** refer to the laws of the mosque. **Rule 908** states that it is preferable not to decorate the mosque with gold, and not to draw the faces of either humans or animals, as these contain spirits. The depiction of things like bushes and flowers, although these have no spirits, is recommended against.

Rules 916 to **941** refer to the laws of calling people to pray, or Azan.

Exact words of the Koran

Nothing in the Koran corresponds to these rules.

Nothing in the Koran corresponds to these rules.

2:187 ... Then complete the fast until nightfall and have no dealings with women while you are secluded at your devotions in the mosques ...

Nothing in the Koran corresponds to these rules.

Shiite Moslem Doctrine (resalah)

Rules 942 to **1164** refer to the laws of exactly how to pray, and that which is allowed and not allowed. For example, **rule 964** says that if a person can stand straight, but places his or her feet too far apart when standing to pray, the prayer is not accepted.

Rules 1165 to **1271** refer to the doubts one might have when praying, and the laws determining how one should deal with them. For example, **rule 1165** deals with the proper manner of prayer. Each prayer is enacted in a number of parts, each of which is accompanied by rules dictating the positions that the worshipper must take. If he feels that he has performed the rituals of prayer in the wrong order, there are certain measures he should take to correct his error, and make his prayer acceptable to God.

Rules 1272 to **1369** govern the prayer of travelers. Persons who are traveling should reduce their prayers from four to two parts. There are eight conditions whereby travelers can reduce their prayers, such as the one named in **rule 1272**, when the journey is more than eight Farsakh (40 kilometers).

Rules 1370 to **1398** refer to making up prayer that is missed or not performed at the correct time. For example, **rule 1371** states that if after the correct time of prayer one realizes that the prayer was void, a compensatory prayer must be made.

Exact words of the Koran

4:43 Those who have brought faith, do not come to pray to God while you are drunk until you know what you are saying...

Nothing in the Koran corresponds to these rules.

4:102 It will not be held against you when you travel out into the world should you shorten prayer, if you fear those who disbelieve may harass you.

Nothing in the Koran corresponds to these rules.

Shiite Moslem Doctrine (resalah)	Exact words of the Koran
Rules 1399 to **1490** cover the laws of praying together. For example, **rule 1402** states that if the leader of a prayer group wishes to pray again, he can do so, so long as the people he leads are different than those in the first group.	Nothing in the Koran corresponds to these rules.
Rules 1507 to **1532** deal with other special prayers. For example, **rule 1513** says that if, on doing the special prayer (Aya), one is in doubt as to how many parts one has prayed, then the prayer is rendered void.	Nothing in the Koran corresponds to these rules.
Rules 1533 to **1549** discuss the laws of getting someone else to perform the prayer that one has not done.	Nothing in the Koran corresponds to these rules.

Shiite Moslem Doctrine (resalah)

Rules 1550 to **1750** are the laws of fasting. **Rule 1584**, for example, says that intercourse while fasting is forbidden, even if the man's penis is only inserted as far as the circumcision mark and he does not ejaculate. **Rule 1585** states that if the insertion does not go as far as the circumcision mark, and no sperm is released, the fast is not voided. **Rule 1678** states that a man who is fasting during the month of Ramadan, and who has intercourse with his own wife by forcing her must pay the penalty for breaking his fast and also pay his wife's penalty.

Exact words of the Koran

2:179 You who believe, fasting has been prescribed for you just as it was prescribed for those before you, so that you may do your duty.

2:180 For a certain number of days; but if someone among you is sick or on a journey, then a number of other days; and those who are not able to do it may be redeemed by feeding a poor man; so whoever does good spontaneously it is better for him; and that you fast is better for you if you know.

2:181 The month of Ramadan is when the Koran was sent down as guidance for mankind and with explanations for guidance, and as a standard. Let any of you who is at home during the month, fast in it; while anyone who is ill or on a journey should [set aside an equal] number of other days. God wants things to be easy for you and does not want any hardship for you...

2:183 It is lawful for you to have intercourse with your wives on the night of the fast: they are garments for you while you are garments for them. God knows how you have been deceiving yourselves, so He has relented towards you and pardoned you. Now [feel free to] frequent them and seek what God has prescribed for you. Eat and drink until the white streak [of dawn] can be distinguished by you from the black thread [of night] at daybreak. Then complete the fast until nightfall and have no dealings with women while you are secluded at your devotions in the mosques. Such are God's limits, so do not attempt to cross them! Thus God explains His signs to mankind so they may do their duty.

Shiite Moslem Doctrine (resalah)

Rules 1751 to **1852** cover the laws of doing business, and the Islamic tax known as "Khomes." For example, **rule 1756** states that if by being frugal during the whole year you are able to save some money then you must pay Khomes on that amount.

Rules 1853 to **2035** refer to the laws of the Islamic tax known as "Zokat." **Rule 1858** states that if a person owns cows, sheep, camels, gold, and silver when he reaches puberty, then he does not have to pay Zokat for that year.

Rules 2036 to **2050** are the laws of pilgrimage. For example, **rule 2038** states that if a woman's pilgrimage to Mecca results in a situation whereby she will find herself short of money, her husband also being unable to provide for her, then she is not required to go.

Exact words of the Koran

8:42 Know that with anything you may acquire as spoils, a fifth of it belongs to God and the messenger, close relatives and orphans, paupers and the wayfarer, if you believe in God and what We have sent down to our servant on the day of distinction, the day when both forces met. God is capable of everything.

2:43 Keep up prayer, pay the welfare tax, and worship along with those who bow their heads.
(The idea of paying part of your earnings to poor people is repeated in many verses).[9]

3:91 In it are clear signs of Abraham's station. Anyone who enters it will be secure. Pilgrimage to the House is a duty imposed on mankind by God, for anyone who can afford a way to do so. Anyone who disbelieves that God is transcendent, beyond the universe.
22:28 Proclaim the pilgrimage among mankind: they will come to you on foot... let them come from every deep ravine.
22:29 ... to bear witness to the advantages they have, and to mention God's name on appointed days over such heads of livestock as He has provided them with. So eat some of it and feed the needy pauper.
22:30 Then let them attend to their grooming, fulfill their vows, and circle round the ancient house.

Shiite Moslem Doctrine (resalah)	Exact words of the Koran
Rules 2051 to **2141** cover the topics of buying and selling. For example, **rule 2058** states that to be on the safe side one should avoid the sale of medicine which contains alcohol in drug stores.	**4:159** ...and took usury although they had been forbidden to, and idly consumed other people's wealth, We have reserved painful torment for those among them who are unbelievers. **4:33** You who believe, do not use up your wealth idly, on one another, unless it is for some business based on mutual consent. Do not kill one another; God has been merciful towards you! **62:11** Yet whenever they see some business or some sport they flock towards it and leave you standing there. Say: "Whatever God has is better than any sport or business. God is the best provider!" **2:282** You who believe, whenever you contract a debt for a stated period, write it down. Let some literate person write between you properly; no literate person should refuse to write it down. Just as God has taught him, so let him write it down, and let the borrower dictate. May he heed God and not omit any part of it.
Rules 2142 to **2172** are the laws of partnership. For example, **rule 2172** says that if one gives his money to another, making a contract that the money should be given to charity in the case of death, then this agreement should be observed.	Nothing in the Koran corresponds to these rules.

Shiite Moslem Doctrine (resalah)	Exact words of the Koran
Rules 2173 to **2227** are the laws of renting. For example, **rule 2179** states that if a mute person uses sign language to indicate whether he rented from someone or is prepared to rent to another, this is acceptable.	Nothing in the Koran corresponds to these rules.
Rules 2228 to **2251** are the rules relating to farming. For example, **rule 2228** says that landowners can let farmers use their land in exchange for a portion of the profit.	Nothing in the Koran corresponds to these rules.
Rules 2252 to **2256** refer to those who cannot assume their own wealth. For example, **rule 2252** says that those who have not yet reached puberty cannot own their own possessions. Puberty is considered to be when the person has grown a substantial amount of hair below the stomach and above the genitals, is able to reach orgasm, or is fifteen years old in the case of a boy, or nine in the case of a girl.	Nothing in the Koran corresponds to these rules.
Rules 2257 to **2272** are laws about doing business, and the power of attorney. **Rule 2258** says that giving power of attorney to someone who lives in another city is permitted, even if the paperwork takes some time to arrive.	Nothing in the Koran corresponds to these rules.
Rules 2273 to **2362** refer to money-lending. **Rule 2273** states that one does not have to say the words: "I am lending you money" when making a loan if the intention is clear. However, the amount involved must be clearly stated.	**2:282** You who believe, whenever you contract a debt for a stated period, write it down.

Shiite Moslem Doctrine (resalah)

Rules 2363 to **2463** are the laws pertaining to marriage. For example, **rule 2394** states that a man may not marry his own cousin if he has previously committed adultery with her mother, while **rule 2395** states that if a man is already married to his cousin when he commits adultery with her mother, his marriage remains valid. **Rule 2405** tells us that, if a man has sex with a boy, then the boy's mother, sister or daughter may not marry him, even if those involved in the act have not yet reached puberty. According to **rule 2406**, if a man is married to another man's mother, sister or daughter, and then has sex with him, the marriage remains legitimate.

Exact words of the Koran

2:220-221 Do not marry women who associate until they believe.

4:26 Do not marry any women whom your fathers have already married, unless this is a thing of the past. It is a shocking act and disgusting, and the worst possible way.

24:32 Marry off any single persons among you...

Shiite Moslem Doctrine (resalah)

Rules 2464 to **2497** are the laws regarding women nursing children. For example, if a woman nurses another woman's child, she cannot marry this woman's husband.

Rules 2498 to **2544** are the laws regulating divorce. For example, **rule 2507** states that if a man wants to divorce his wife, and for some reason she misses a period, he cannot divorce her until they have been apart for three months.

Exact words of the Koran

2:233 Mothers should breast-feed their children for two full years, provided they want to complete the nursing. The fathers must support women and clothe them properly. Yet no person is charged with more than he can cope with. No mother should be made to suffer because of her child, nor any father because of his child. An heir is the same in that respect. If they both prefer to wean when they agree on terms and consult together, it should not be held against them; so if you want to find a wet-nurse for your children, it should not be held against you, provided you hand over whatever you may have given in all decency. Heed God and know that God is observant of anything you do.

2:231 Once you divorce women, and they have reached the end of their waiting period, then either retain them in all decency or part from them decently. Do not retain them just to be spiteful.
2:232 Whenever you divorce women and they have reached the end of their waiting period, do not hinder them from marrying their [former] husbands if they have agreed to do so...
2:238 If you divorce women before you have had contact with them and have already assigned them a living, then [give them] half of the [dowry]...

Shiite Moslem Doctrine (resalah)

Rules 2545 to **2563** refer to laws regarding oppression. **Rule 2551** says that if two people take something away from another person by force, each is liable for half, even though each could have taken the whole thing for himself.

Rules 2564 to **2582** refer to cases when money or other valuables are found. **Rule 2564** says that if valuables are found without an address to which to return them, they should be donated to charity on behalf of the unknown owner.

Exact words of the Koran

4:61 ...Whenever you judge between people, you should judge with justice...
4:134 O you who believe! Be maintainers of justice, bearers of witness for God's sake ...
5:11 You who believe, stand up for God, as witnesses for justice, and do not let ill-will toward any folk incriminate you so that you swerve from dealing justly. Be just ...
6:153 ... Whenever you speak, be just even though it concerns a close relative.
7:180 Some of those whom We have created form a nation which guides [mankind] by means of the truth, and because of it they act justly.
16:92 God commands justice, kindness and giving.

Nothing in the Koran corresponds to these rules.

Shiite Moslem Doctrine (resalah)	Exact words of the Koran
Rules 2583 to **2614** are rules regarding slaughtering or hunting animals to eat. For example, **rule 2585** tells us that a wild animal that may be eaten can only be consumed if it is capable of running or flying away. Thus, baby animals or birds may not be eaten. If a hunter kills both an adult and its young with one bullet, only the adult creature may be consumed.	**5:6** They will ask you what has been made permissible for them. Say: "It is lawful for you to eat wholesome things. You have trained hounds and birds of prey to catch. You have trained them to do something just as God has taught you. So eat anything they may catch for you, and mention God's name over it." Heed God, God is swift in reckoning. **5:1** You who believe fulfill any contract. Any livestock animals are permitted you, except for what has already been listed. What is not permitted for you is game in the month in which it is forbidden. God judges anything He wishes. **5:6** ...when you hunt, eat the meat and then thank God.
Rules 2615 to **2621** are laws pertaining to fish and fishing. For example, **rule 2615** states that one must not eat a fish unless it has a shell on its body.	The Koran tells us that we may eat all sea animals.

Shiite Moslem Doctrine (resalah)

Rules 2622 to **2623** are the rules regarding hunting grasshoppers. **Rule 2622** states that one may eat a dead grasshopper which has been caught either in the hand or with a tool. It's not necessary that the person who caught it be Moslem, or that they say the name of God. However, if an atheist catches the grasshopper it may not be eaten, even if it was alive when caught. **Rule 2623** states that it is forbidden to eat a grasshopper which has not developed wings and cannot therefore fly.

Rules 2624 to **2639** are the rules governing eating and drinking. For example, **rule 2631** states that it is not recommended to eat the meat of a horse or donkey, while he who commits a sexual act with one of these animals must take them out of town and sell them.

Rule 2732 explains that if one commits a sexual act with a cow, sheep or camel, their waste becomes unclean, drinking their milk is forbidden and the animal must be immediately killed and burned, while he who had sex with it must pay the price of the animal to its owner. [This is another one of those rules that really made me scratch my head and wonder about the warped minds that imagine such things!]

Exact words of the Koran

Nothing in the Koran corresponds to these rules.

The Koran tells us simply to eat or drink without wastage, and without over-eating.

Nothing in the Koran corresponds to this rule.

Shiite Moslem Doctrine (resalah)

Rule 2644 tells us that drinking alcohol is a sin, that some have said that it is the biggest sin of all, while **rule 2635** instructs us that it is every Moslem's duty to give water and food to another Moslem who is close to dying because of a lack of either.

Exact words of the Koran

4:46 You who believe, do not attempt to pray while you are drunk, until you know what you are saying.

2:216 They will ask you about liquor and gambling. Say: "In each of them there lies serious vice as well as some benefits for mankind. Yet their vice is greater than their usefulness." They may ask you what to spend. Say: "As much as you can spare!" Thus God explains His verses to you so that you may meditate.

5:92 You who believe, liquor and gambling, idols and raffles, are only the filthy work of Satan; turn aside from it so that you may prosper.

5:93 Satan only wants to stir up enmity and jealousy among you by means of liquor and gambling, and to hinder you from remembering God and from praying. So will you stop?

Rules 2640 to **2675** are the laws of "Nazr" and deal-making. "Nazr" is a term used to describe the act of doing something charitable, or another type of good deed, for the sake of making God happy, or promising God to give up some bad habit. **Rule 2644** tells us that a married woman is not allowed to promise God anything, as a Nazr, without the permission of her husband.

2:273 God knows any expenses you may have incurred, or any promise you may have sworn. Wrongdoers will have no supporters.

Shiite Moslem Doctrine (resalah)	Exact words of the Koran
Rules 2676 to **2693** are the laws governing acts of charity. For example, **rule 2683** says that charity given to those who are not yet born is not considered acceptable.	**35:26** The ones who recite God's book, keep up prayer and spend something both secretly and publicly from whatever He has provided for them, can hope for a business which will never slacken.[10]

Clearly, the issue of giving charity to the poor is one of the few cases where the religious leaders do not discuss a vast range of laws. Unsurprisingly, however, this is a point which is strongly stressed by God, who provides us with a lengthy list of commands regarding the importance of giving. The same is true of the Bible. Religious authorities busy themselves with worrying over minute details of matters such as the proper way to wash the hands. But when it comes to the important issues, they have little or nothing to say.

Shiite Moslem Doctrine (resalah)	Exact words of the Koran
Rules 2694 to **2790** are the rules of inheritance. **Rule 2691** says that if one donates a carpet to a charity of some kind, it cannot later be used for prayer in the mosque.	**2:241** For those of you who pass away leaving [widowed] spouses, a will means making provision for a year without having them leave [home]... **4:12** God instructs you concerning your children: a son should have a share equivalent to that of two daughters. If the women [left behind] are more than two, then two-thirds of whatever he leaves belong to them ... **4:13-14** You will have (as inheritance) half of anything your wives leave, provided they have no child... **5:105** You who believe, testimony should be taken by you whenever death appears for one of you; at the time for drawing up any will, two of you who are fair-minded.
Rules 2791 to **2825** are the laws regarding advising others to do good, and refraining from doing bad. For example, **2794** says that if you think you will encourage someone to break a law by remaining silent then you must speak out. This is especially true in the case of religious leaders.	**22:42** Those who, if We established them in the land, would keep up prayer and pay the welfare tax, command what is proper and forbid debauchery. God holds the destiny of things!
Rules 2826 to **2835** are the laws of defense. For example, rule **2826** says that if an enemy attacks the land of the Moslems, all Moslems are obliged to defend it.	This topic has already been discussed in some detail in chapter eight, above.

Shiite Moslem Doctrine (resalah)	Exact words of the Koran
Rules 2835 to **2897** are the laws of things that relate to our time. For example, **rule 2858** says that isn't forbidden for companies to give gifts or other objects to customers using a lottery system.	Nothing in the Koran corresponds to these rules.

It's easy to see that the word of God has been utterly changed by the religious leaders who claim to be able to interpret it. In this perverted form, it is presented to uneducated Moslems all over the world. Generations of religious leaders who have passed on the teachings of their predecessors have taken their toll on the integrity of the Moslem tradition—and this is also true of the other great religious faiths. For example, Christ was faced with the dilemma of dealing with Jewish religious leaders who had similarly distorted the Judaic religion. He describes the situation in the Gospel of Mark, chapter 7, verses 2 to 23 (emphasis mine):

Now when they saw some of his disciples eat bread with defiled, that is, with unwashed hands, they found fault. For the Pharisees and all the Jews do not eat unless they wash their hands in a special way, in accordance with the tradition of the elders. When they come from the marketplace, they do not eat unless they wash. And there are many other things which they have received and hold, like the washing of cups, pitchers, copper vessels, and couches. Then the Pharisees and scribes asked him: "Why do your disciples not walk according to the tradition of the elders, but eat bread with unwashed hands?" He answered and said to them: "Well, did Isaiah prophesy of you hypocrites, as it is written: 'This people honors Me with their lips, but their heart is far from Me. And in vain they worship Me, teaching as doctrines the commandments of men.'" [Note carefully that this verse says "in vain they worship me," bearing in mind the terrorists who kill in vain, thinking that they are doing so for God.] "For laying aside the commandment of God, you hold the tradition of men—the washing of pitchers and cups, and many other such things you do." He said to them: "All too well you reflect the commandment of God, that you may keep your tradition. For Moses said: 'Honor your father and your mother' and: 'He who curses father or mother, let him be put to death.' But you say: 'If a man says to his father or mother, whatever profit you might have received from me is Corban'—(that is, a gift to God), and you no longer let him do anything for his father or his mother, *making the word of God of no effect through your tradition which you have handed down. And many such things you do.*" When he had called all the multitude to himself, he said to them: "Hear me, everyone, and understand: there is nothing that enters a man from outside which can defile him; but the things which come out of him, those are the things that defile a man. If anyone has ears to hear, let him hear!" When he had entered a house away from the crowd, his disciples asked him concerning the parable. So he said to them: "Are you thus without understanding also? Do you not perceive that whatever enters a man from outside cannot defile him, because it does not enter his heart but his stomach, and is eliminated, thus purifying all foods?" And he said: "What comes out of a man, that defiles a man. For from within, out of the heart of men, proceed evil thoughts, adulteries, fornication, murders, theft, covetousness, wickedness, deceit, lewdness, an evil eye, blasphemy, pride, foolishness. All these evil things come from within and defile a man."

In the Koran, too, it says many times that no man should try to replace God's word with a word of their own, saying that the men who do so are the worst of creatures:

"… Do not sell God's words for any price…And do not mix up the truth with the falsehood, nor hide the truth while you know it."

"But those who did injustice by changing the word [of God] to another word which had been spoken to them, so We send down to those who did this injustice a punishment from the sky because they transgressed."

"Do you then wish that they would believe in you, and a group of them indeed heard the word of God, then altered it after they had understood it, and they know [this]."

"And there are among them illiterates who know not the book but only lies, and they are of all doubts, therefore woe, to those who write the book with their hands and then say: "This is from God, so that they may take for it a small price; therefore woe to them for what their hands have written and woe to them for what they earn from it."

" ...Who is more unjust than someone who hides some evidence from God which He holds?..."

" ... Nevertheless a group of them hide the truth even though they know it."

"God curses those who hide whatever We send down as explanations and guidance, once We have explained it to mankind in the book, and cursers will cure them. Except for those who repent, and explain [what they hide from people]..."

"He [the devil] merely orders you to commit evil and shocking deeds, and to say what you do not know about God."

"Those who hide what God has sent down in the book and sell it for a small worldly price. They do not eat but the fire in their bellies. God will not speak to them on the Resurrection Day nor will He purify them; they will have painful torment! Those are the ones who have purchased error instead of guidance, and torment instead of forgiveness. Why do they insist on facing the fire? That is because God has sent the book down with the truth, while those who disagree about the book go much too far in dissension."[11]

The perversion of Islam did not happen overnight. It was a gradual process, occurring over a period of 1300 years following the death of the Prophet Muhammad. By now, the religious tradition of Islam has become unspeakably altered.

It is beyond the scope of this book to discuss all the false doctrine that has become a part of contemporary Shiite religious tradition. However, we can examine some of those aspects of the doctrine that are particularly disruptive in the lives of the Shiites. Some examples are as follows (teachings of Shiite leaders are on the left, extracts from the Koran on the right):

When a Moslem hears the name "Muhammad," he should say: "Peace be upon Muhammad, and all his descendents."	God and His angels praise the prophet. You who believe, praise him and greet him properly. [12]

Religious leaders insist that people should say "peace be upon Muhammad and his descendents" every single time they hear the prophet's name. Similarly, these words should be written when his name occurs in writing. When they themselves write books, they preface Muhammad's name with those words. Neglecting to do so in conversation with a Moslem person is considered a very great disrespect to Muhammad. A normal conversation is greatly disrupted every time the prophet's name is mentioned.

When there is a power outage in a Moslem person's house, everyone in the household yells: "Peace be upon Muhammad and his descendents," repeating these words when the power is restored.

When people are on public transport or in public places, it's common for someone to shout "Salavat!" which means: "say 'peace be upon Muhammad and his descendents.'" Once everyone has done so, it is very common for the same person to yell: "Say it again, and louder!" The third time, they shout: "Can't you scream?"

Many Shiites have witnessed situations in which two people are on the verge of fighting when someone shouts "Salavat!" to stop them, following which everyone says: "Peace be upon Muhammad and his descendents." The same occurs in the case of simple arguments.

It is also common practice to take a *tasbead*, which is a string of one hundred beads, and say "Salavat" one hundred times, keeping track with the beads. (Someone needs to quote Jesus' words as they are recorded in the Bible where he reminded us that God understands us the first time! It would also be worth mentioning that God is not deaf.)

Above all, the Koran says, no one should be praised more than God—even Muhammad. In the Koran, we learn of an occasion on which God became angry because the people esteemed Muhammad too highly:

"...and when they come to you they greet you with a greeting with which God does not greet you..." [13]

It is impossible to have a normal conversation on the topic of

Muhammad with any Moslem in a mosque, because there are constant interruptions by people saying: "Peace be upon Muhammad and his descendents," every single time his name is mentioned. Unfortunately, similar rules are observed by Shiite Moslems with respect to Muhammad's *imams*, who are asked to intercede with God on their behalf to make their lives better. They praise them so much that they exceed the limits set by the Koran, which says: "Do not praise your religious people in the way you should praise God."

"...and some of us shall not take others for lords besides God..."

"They have taken their knowledgeable once and their religious leaders for lords besides God..."[14]

| Muhammad and his youngest daughter and the twelve apostles descended from that daughter are sinless. | Nothing in the Koran corresponds to this. |

The Shiite Moslems, as well as most Sunnis, believe that Muhammad was without sin, while the Shiite extend this to include his daughter and apostles. And yet, in the Koran, God cites a number of occasions on which Muhammad committed a sin:

"God pardon you! Why did you give them leave until those who spoke the truth had become manifest to you and you knew the liars?"

"...and you feared men, and you should have feared God."

"O prophet! Why do you forbid (yourself) that which God has made lawful for you; you seek to please your wives; and God is forgiving, merciful."[15]

On one occasion, God even warns Muhammad, telling him to be careful not to repeat the sin. Muhammad had been worried about what his wives thought of him, and God told him that He should fear only Him before his wives.

Elsewhere, Muhammad gave permission to a hypocritical man not to join the war against God's enemies. God, knowing that the man was hypocritical, became angry with Muhammad. He said that, being aware that the man was a hypocrite and two-faced, Muhammad should not have granted him this permission.[16]

| Muhammad was able to predict the future. | Nothing in the Koran corresponds to this. |

In the Koran, God says:

"Muhammad, tell the people that you do not know the future, and that if you did, you would never let any harm come to you, and you would be wealthy. But you are a common man with no education, and you have been chosen to tell my words to the people."[17]

| Muhammad and his apostles can help a people receive forgiveness from God interceding on their behalf. | Nothing in the Koran corresponds to this. |

Shiite Moslems often ask Muhammad's *imams* for help more than they ask God. And when they kill animals, they kill them in the name of the *imams*. Their reasoning is that they are honoring the *imams* because they are godly, and God loves them. This is a practice that is strongly forbidden in the Koran, and which is discussed often.

It is very common among Shiite Moslems to say: "Ali help us," when they lift heavy things. When they drink water they say: "Peace be upon Hussein." This is closer to worshipping idols than worshipping God, and has been accomplished with the aid of the application of *ahadith*. The darkness of tradition has blinded the light of the Koran.[18]

| Cigarettes are acceptable. | Nothing in the Koran corresponds to this. |

Smoking is a common practice among religious leaders. Bear in mind that the tobacco cartels in Iran pay substantial taxes to them. Of course they don't forbid something that has been medically proven to cause serious damage to the health! Many religious leaders are known to smoke and many also consume opium.

Men should not wear gold—if they do, their prayers will not be accepted.	The Koran states that one should wear jewels—and in other verses states that gold is considered a jewel[19]—and try to look good.[20]

Although the Koran clearly states that one should take the jewels made from resources created by God and use them for adornment, the *ahadith* say that only women can wear gold—with the exception of white gold which men are allowed to wear.

Christians are impure. If one comes into physical contact with a Christian, one must wash.	It is allowed to eat the food of Christians[21]—some Christians are so pure that they will be richly rewarded by God.[22]

If they touch a Christian with a wet hand, many Moslems go and wash their hand three times by dipping it in water. They also recommend washing the hands seven times after touching a dog.[23]

The Bible is wrong, even when it gives simple, beautiful instructions like the following Lord's Prayer: *Our Father who art in Heaven, hallowed be Thy name. Thy kingdom come, Thy will be done on Earth, as it is in Heaven. Give us this day our daily bread. And forgive us our debts, as we forgive our debtors. And lead us not into temptation but deliver us from the evil. For Thine is the kingdom the power and the glory forever. AMEN.*	In the Koran, we learn that the Bible was from God and should be believed, with the exception of those parts that say that Jesus is the son of God or is God himself (See chapter 9, section 7, above).

The most famous Shiite religious leader, Ayatollah Tabatabaie, is well known for his translation and interpretation of the Koran. He is well respected in Ghom, the center of Shiite Islamic studies, and is a famous philosopher. He studies everything intelligently, and usually opts to interpret things logically. However, at some point, his prejudice against Christians took over, and reason left him. His interpretation of the above prayer is as follows:

"Our Father in Heaven means that God is in Heaven, and by this [the Christians] mean that God is only in the skies. This is wrong because God is everywhere. Then they say: 'Hallowed be your name'. This is a very low prayer, and doesn't even show basic respect. It's like praying for God to be well. They [the Christians] say that they hope that His rule will remain stable on Earth as it is in the skies. Why are the Christians requesting this on God's behalf? It sounds more like a political slogan than a prayer. Then they ask their God to give them their daily bread, in return for which they will forgive those who commit sins against them. And ... God should in return forgive them for their sin. What right do the Christians have to bargain with God? The Christians continue their prayer by asking God not to test them, but to deliver them from temptations. This is an impossibility, because we should be tested in this world, and untested faith is meaningless."[24]

Only an ignorant, prejudiced person can believe Ayatollah Tabatabaie's statements about this very beautiful prayer, which was given to Christians by God through Jesus Christ.

No matter how good a Jew or Christian is, he will still go to Hell because he is not a Moslem.	Regardless of whether one is Jew, Christian, Moslem, or undecided, the person who believes in God and does good will be saved and go to heaven.[25]

Unlike most religious texts, the Koran says that even non-believers will not go to Hell if they can justify their disbelief in a reasonable way. The Koran even describes non-believers as having to possess certain characteristics if they are to go to Hell, including mistreating orphans, just as believers are supposed to have certain characteristics.[26] Nonetheless, God instructs Moslems to tell Jews and Christians that we are all believers, sharing much in common since the times of the prophet Abraham.

The Koran also states that if a Christian or Jew accepts Muhammad as a prophet of God, he will be rewarded twice over. By this, God is stating that He understands that it is hard for a believer to leave his own creed and accept a new one.[27]

Rule 2594 says that animals to be eaten must be slaughtered while the name of God is pronounced by a Moslem. If a Christian says the name of God before slaughtering an animal, it is unfit to eat.

Certain animals—cattle, camels and sheep—were created for humans to eat, so they may do so, reminding themselves of God.[28]

It is amazing to see how the wealthy make business out of religion. Many stores advertise *halal* meat—*halal* referring to the way in which the animal was killed. In the Koran, God stresses:

"If I have forbidden you to eat anything, bring the book and show me where I have said that."[29]

It also says:

"All things that seem to you to be pure can be eaten. All bad things, that seem impure, should not be eaten."[30]

Again, it says that Moslems should forbid those things that God has already made good, adding that everything edible may be eaten, with the exception of a few named things—blood, swine and animals that were killed by suffocation or in the name of one who is not God.[31] However, Moslems should not eat unless they bless their food in the name of God—a practice also followed by Christians and Jews. In the New Testament, God gives the same message.[32]

Show love only to Moslems.	**41:34** A good deed and an evil deed are not alike: repel bad with good, so one who is your enemy is like he is your best friend. **41:35** Yet no one will be given this unless the patient, and no one will be given this unless one of high fortune.
One of the traditional prayers is to invoke the curse of God on one group of people or another.	Invariably, the Koran tells people to pray respectfully without going to ridiculous lengths.

Shiite religious leaders encourage the faithful to use a prayer that curses three of the figures who are well respected by the Sunni. Many prayers curse these three men, and wish death to those who follow them. Another prayer curses the *imams* descended from Hussein. This practice clearly encourages hatred between the two principal Moslem groups.

In his introduction to the interpretation of the Koran, Ayatollah Tabatabaie[33] says:

"How can the Koran not be easily understood by an ordinary man, when the Koran itself claims that it is very clear in order that humans comprehend?"[34]

God said to Muhammad, "I made these words very easy to understand," saying:

"We have made the Koran easy for guidance, will anyone be guided? [Repeated four times]"[35]

So, says the Ayatollah, how does anyone dare to use their knowledge to interpret the Koran, for doing so is like trying to light the sun with a flashlight? He further asks how the word of God could seem to mean one thing, and later be interpreted to mean the exact opposite.[36]

Dogs are impure. If anyone touches one of these animals, he must wash seven times.[37]	In at least one place in the Koran, prophets are described as owning dogs.[38]

Many Moslem people characteristically mistreat dogs, as if they were creations of the devil rather than of God. However, the Koran refers to dogs that were owned by the prophets. In most Moslem countries, religious leaders have caused Moslem people to hate dogs. These unfortunate animals are often starved and abused.

Only fish with special scales on their skin may be eaten.[39]	The Koran says that one can eat any creature from the sea.[40]

Although the Koran states that all marine creatures may be eaten, the traditional laws say that only creatures with scales may be eaten.

One cannot shorten the obligatory prayers when reaching one's destination after a journey, unless one is to stay there for more than ten days, as well as fulfilling many other conditions.[41]	While traveling one may shorten one's prayer if one is fearful of being pursued by an enemy.[42]

Shiite Moslem leaders believe that, if a person is traveling, they should shorten their prayers, and should not use the full prayers, unless they plan to stay at their destination for ten days or more. This creates a lot of difficulty, because many Moslems will not travel back and forth from a given place of business, and risk shortening their prayers. For example, my father wanted us to stay in our village, which was twenty miles from Tehran, in the summer. My mother wanted to fast during Ramadan. The religious leaders said that we should come to the border of the town to perform the noon and afternoon prayer so that the prayer and fast would be accepted. My father, not a very religious man, would regularly curse his wife, and his religion, as he drove her to and from the border of the town every day during the thirty days of Ramadan. All the Koran says on this matter is that Moslems who pray may shorten their prayer if they are fearful of their enemies! This was a rule written at a time of incessant tribal warfare.

A man who forces his wife to have sex during a time of fasting must afterwards feed one hungry person as penance for his sin, and one for the sin of his wife.[43]	Nothing in the Koran corresponds to this rule.

The violation of women has been a right of men throughout the history of Islam, except perhaps during Muhammad's lifetime. How could anybody in their right mind justify rape, and punish it with a fine equivalent to a couple of dollars to be given to the poor?

Before eating, one should say: "In the name of God." However, if one is slaughtering an animal, one should turn it towards Mecca, give it water, say "with the name of God" and cut only the front vein on the neck. If you kill animals in any other way, they may not be eaten. If this procedure is performed by a non-Moslem, the meat remains inedible.[44]	When one eats anything one must remind oneself of God.[45]
Prayers should be offered in the name of the imams of Muhammad. People may kiss the hands of the religious leaders.	The Koran clearly states that religious leaders should not be aggrandized, and that the people should not be overly humble towards them.[46] This is extended to include even those who talk about watching the Prophet Muhammad at prayer with excessive excitement.[47]

The Koran says that one should never praise anyone in the manner in which they should praise God. Religious leaders allow people to kiss their hands and even their feet, exempting themselves from these rules.

Excessive praise is generally used when talking about religious leaders. For example, Khomeni's *resalah* is prefaced:

> "Religious supreme martyrdom, the supreme, the most powerful, the man who broke all oppressions and the idols of our time, the helper of our generation, the ayatollah, the greatest leader, the spirit of God. Ayatollah Khomeni, the sacred spirit."

As I went through all the laws of Islam, comparing the teachings of the Koran with those of the religious leaders, my sense of horror at the vast disparities between the two grew and grew. How did Moslem religious leaders manage to pervert God's law from the message clearly given in the Koran to something completely different? *Why* did they do this? Much the same has happened over the years in Judaism and Christianity. In historic times, the laws of Moses were changed so much that, when Jesus came, most religious leaders were aghast at his message.

> But Jesus told them, "You have taken away the key of knowledge. Not only would you not enter yourselves, you would hinder those who were entering."[48]

These are strong words indeed.

Reading the extracts from Moslem rule books and the Koran, any non-Moslem will agree that the original meaning of the text has been altered beyond belief. However, Moslem leaders and ordinary Moslems will usually argue, against reason, that the laws were given to us by the Prophet Muhammad, or at least one of his apostles, and passed down through the generations. Most faithful Moslems will blindly argue for the point of view of their religious leaders, because they have become unable to think for themselves. They can justify anything. I was shocked, when reading the *resalah* or rule-book of Khomeni, to find a rule which started as follows:

> "If a woman is having sex with her husband, and half way through she realizes that the man she is having sex with is not her husband, but that she made a mistake, then ..."

How can such a rule find its way into a religious document at all? I spoke about this very issue with various Shiite Moslems, and most of them tried to justify the existence of such laws. One even told me that they demonstrated the courage of Moslem religious leaders, saying that Christians don't have the bravery necessary to write about such difficult situations.

"Come on," I said, with incredulity, "these things just don't happen."

"They do," he insisted, and told me that just a few days earlier, a woman he knew told him that she'd been approached by a man who said that he thought she was his wife.

"She was upset," he informed me, "but thank God, she had the rules and knew exactly what to do."

Most of the Moslems to whom I spoke, however, were unaware of the more ludicrous of the rules from the *resalah,* and no one of my acquaintance has ever heard of anybody committing any of the unspeakable acts that the rule book seems to suggest are commonplace.

Listening to this sort of nonsense almost discouraged me from writing this book. But I feel that, as a Moslem, it is my duty to put these words into print, regardless of the outcome.

(ON(LVDING NOTE)

There is a famous saying among Moslems which relates that if God were to enumerate the number of true believers in Him at any moment in time he would not need more than ten fingers to count them all. For years, I considered this to be an exaggeration. Then I read that part of the Bible in which Jesus says:

> "And Jesus said unto them, Because of your unbelief: for verily I say unto you, If ye have faith as a grain of mustard seed, ye shall say unto this mountain, 'Remove hence to yonder place,' and it shall remove; and nothing shall be impossible unto you."[1]

It's easy to see that, in this world, the self-proclaimed religious leaders are lacking something important, and that is a single drop of faith.

Another story from Moslem tradition tells of a tribe that was suffering from extreme drought. No matter how hard everyone—including the religious leaders—prayed, the rain just didn't come. There was a rich man in that tribe, and as he was walking and wondering to himself why God did not answer the prayers of all these people, in the distance he saw a poor black man who knelt beneath a tree and said to God: "O Lord, they have suffered enough. Please spare them and give them rain." Clouds appeared immediately, and rain fell upon the land. The rich man was surprised by what he had seen, and he followed the black man to see where he went. He entered a house, and the rich man knocked on the door and asked who the black man who had just entered the house was. The inhabitants answered that he was a slave, and the rich man immediately offered to buy him. When the slave heard this, he answered that the master of the house had released him from his servitude long before but that he chose to stay because he was a good master and treated him well.

"But I have seen your power," the rich man said, "God listened to your request and sent the rain when you asked for it. I want to buy you so that I can be your servant and you can be my master."

"You saw how God listened to me?" the slave asked.

"Why, yes," the rich man said, "I saw the whole thing."

The slave looked at the sky and said, "Lord, I did not want anyone to know about how you have blessed me, and now that this is revealed I have no wish to live any longer." He fell and died before the rich man's eyes.

Now, this story is a legend, so it's unlikely that it's literally true, but the message it contains is very meaningful. Evangelists and other braggarts and boastful religious leaders who seek fortune instead of God need to listen to this story. If their claims to great powers are really true, and they can actually move mountains, cure people and perform every type of miraculous act they should be modest about their gifts, and not allow their relationship with God to be revealed so easily. For if it were revealed, they might become famous on earth and receive worldly goods for their gift, making them vulnerable to temptation, lies and conceit. The truly godly man or woman has no interest in things of this world, and does not want to exchange his or her faith for fame, power, and money.

I have spent the last seven years of my life studying the Koran in detail, and to a lesser extent the Bible, and comparing their messages to that of the religious leaders who minister to the people. Nothing in either book instructs us to form cliques of our religious peers and set ourselves up as rivals of the other groups. Instead, they both preach tolerance, respect and mutual love.

Many honest and well-meaning people say that they are confused. There are so many religions in the world claiming to be the right path to God—how can one decide? Who can be believed? When the dark clouds that gather above the heads of the religious leaders threaten to obscure the light; when the road to God becomes so narrow and twisting that you don't know which way to go; when your mind is pulled in all directions until you are almost ready to give up the quest, then prepare yourself to let your heart take charge. The answer to these questions, which perplex so many, is more simple than anyone can imagine. The truth lies in your own conscience. Only you can show yourself the right way to live. Are you going to steal because you do not know which religion to choose? Are you going to kill innocent people, or torture and mutilate yourself or others because you do not have a religious authority who tells you what to do? If your answer is "no," then no matter which book of God you are following, whether the Torah, the Bible, or the Koran, you are a godly person, and if there is an afterlife, you will be rewarded for your actions and your actions alone. The God of the Torah, the Bible and the Koran will not be interested in which church or mosque or synagogue you attended. The world may seem to offer so many options that you may become confused as to the proper way to live a righteous life. Treat others as you would like them to treat you and you will be rewarded.

That which prevents many of the educated people of the world from believing in God is the society which we have created for ourselves. Educated men and women look around and see a world divided by hate, with curses spat from the mouths of the religious leaders and their followers who lead the rabble. Reasonably, many educated people want nothing to do with faith or with the faithful, as they see the destruction that religion brings. When they reject religion, I have to agree with their choice wholeheartedly. But still, I say that in rejecting religion, it is not necessary to cease believing in God and doing good deeds.

Religion is a dangerous tool, and in the hands of dangerous people, it becomes a weapon of destruction. But in the hands of the good, it is a tool that can be used for the betterment of the world.

A friend of mine once asked me, "Why does God need people to pray to Him so much? Is his self-esteem so low that he needs constant thanks?"

"Would you thank me if I gave you a million dollars?" I wanted to know.

"Of course," he said.

"But if you had lost one of your hands, wouldn't you give back that same million dollars to have it returned to you?"

"Of course," he said again.

"Well," I told him, "not only have you been given an unlimited amount from God, but by thanking Him you will learn to recognize all you have, and you will become a better person. God doesn't need you to thank Him. His powers are unlimited. But by thanking God, you make yourself stronger, and you learn to appreciate your own talents, life and gifts more than you ever could alone."

Deciding to love God the right way rather than following the teachings of religious leaders is a difficult decision to make, even though it is the correct one. Those who opt not to participate in tribal hatreds, be they Jews, Moslems or Christians, will be cast from their group of believers, and probably from their families, too.

The lands which have been most paralyzed and held back by contempt are the Moslem nations. Moslem people inhabit lands which are beautiful and rich in resources. Their culture has an ancient history of learning, and is supposed to be based upon the Koran. But still these countries remain poor and underdeveloped, the people uneducated and oppressed. Why?

Because their religious leaders teach them to despise other religious groups, and to shun cooperation with Christian and Jewish lands.

Instead of preaching forgiveness, religious leaders on both sides fuel the conflict by assuring their murderous flocks that they are acting in the name of God. And as long as hatred is taught by one generation to the next it will grow in strength and venom. But God's glory will be upon the generation that calls a halt, by choosing love instead of hate. These pioneers will be despised by their peers, and may even be killed by them, but their sacrifice will help us all to move towards an open, tolerant world.

From my home in the United States, I have chosen to abandon the trappings of formal religion in exchange for the true message of the Koran and the other great books of God. But I am not a religious leader, and many of my fellow Moslems wish to dismiss what I say. They will call me "Jew-lover" or "Christian-lover" as if these were terrible things to be. They will say that I have been Americanized and that I am ignorant. But I am happy, because I know that I am doing my best to follow the Koran as God intended, and this happiness is far more rewarding than the approval of a religious leader or my peers. I do love Jews, as God loved them. As the Koran says, God loved Jews enough to make them excel above all others:

"…and I made you excel all nations of the world…"[2]

I love Christians, too, as the Koran has said that devout Christians try to exceed each other in doing good. And yes, I definitely love all Moslems, fanatic and non-fanatic, American and non-American.

I cannot say, "Death to America" as I was raised to do, for America gave me more than any country ever could. I cannot say "Death to Jews" even if they take my land, for that land cannot go to the other world with me. I will not say "Death to those Moslems who do not agree with me completely," because I am not God, to decide who should die and who should live. But, as He commanded me to love, I will. For His command in the Koran is everything to me.

My intention in writing and publishing this book was to make of it a call to my brothers and sisters—a call to change. Let's learn from the tragic lessons of history and stop hating. Let's learn from the example of the most just nation that humanity has created to date. Let's learn from the United States of America.

The devil appears in many forms, and frequently he is wearing the robes of Moslem religious authority. If you listen to him, he will convince you to kill thousands in the name of God and to wage war on God's behalf.

In the Koran it says that on the Day of Judgment, everyone will be lined up in front of their prophets: the Moslems with Muhammad, the Jews with Moses and the Christians with Jesus, and each person will be judged according to whether or not he or she obeyed the rules given to them by God in their holy book:

"How then shall it be, when We bring forward from every nation a witness, and bring you [Muhammad] as a witness against those?"[3]

"...[Jesus] will be a witness to them [Christians] on the resurrection day..."[4]

"Every nation has a messenger, once their messenger has come, judgment will be passed upon them in all fairness and they will not be wronged."[5]

"And you shall see every nation kneeling down; every nation shall be called to its book: today you shall be rewarded for what you did."

" ...We wrote what you did... "

"Then as to those who believed and did good, their Lord will make them enter into His mercy; that is the manifest achievement."

"As to those who disbelieved: What! Were not My communications recited to you? But you were proud and you were a guilty people."[6]

If you are a Jew, and you have never read the Torah, or a Christian who has never read the Bible, or a Moslem who has never read the Koran, what will you say? That, choosing ignorance, you listened to your religious leader and did his bidding? That you did not love God enough to take His book and read it for yourself?

The Moslems of today must stop imagining that God is happy with them, and with what they have accomplished since the death of Muhammad. They should not suppose that the corruption which affected Christianity and Judaism after the death of those groups' prophets has not also affected them. In the Koran, God speaks harshly of Moslem hypocrites, and separates them from true Moslems. He also deals separately with good and bad Jews and Christians, describing as "good" those who are faithful to the teachings of their books (the Torah and the Bible) rather than the traditions of man. We must apply the same criteria to contemporary Moslems. Those who blindly follow the ridiculous interpretations of so-called religious leaders will have to learn to lay aside their trust in men and live instead according to the rules of the Koran, and nothing else.

The Koran criticizes Moslems who are hypocrites and do not pray with honest hearts, much more than those who deny that God exists:

"Have you seen someone who rejects religion?
That is a person who pushes the orphan aside
And does not promote feeding the needy.
So woe to the worshippers
Who are unmindful of their prayers.
Who do (good) in order to be seen.
And withhold the necessaries of life."[7]

God encourages Moslems to do good even to the people who treat them badly, and to love their enemies.

Americans have been blessed by God for their hard work and their open-mindedness. They have created a free society. Now, more than ever, they must be careful not to allow the forces of evil to destroy this justice. America has been attacked by misled religious fanatics. America should never cease to love, for this love is what has opened the eyes of people like me.

Today, more than ever, religious leaders need to serve the people the way God intended. It is the government's job to make and enforce law, not the religious leaders'. The religious leaders' job is simply to guide those who seek God. The opposite of this happened in Iran following the revolution and ordinary people in that country are suffering because of it every day.

If the religious leaders try to be anything other than a reminder of God's message, they will destroy all His work, carried out through the ages. God's angry message to the Jewish leaders, passed to them through Jesus Christ, made this very clear.

When animals fight, they follow their instincts and fight for survival. God's message to us is that we should also observe this rule. Human beings are able to overcome any animal with the technology that their intelligence has created, but fighting bullets with stones, as is the case in Palestine today, is beneath even the dignity of beasts. The Prophet Muhammad accepted humiliation until he had enough force to fight back with dignity. Until then, he and his followers hid from their aggressors. Once their strength had grown, they attacked those who had harmed and killed innocent Moslem people. When their enemies surrendered, as occurred in Mecca, peace was made, even when the enemy had been outstandingly cruel, and responsible for the deaths of innocent Moslems (and even the wives of the followers of Muhammad, as also occurred in Mecca). God's law was that peace should be established, and this is how it was. Muhammad fought only when it was necessary to protect innocent lives. He ordered that not even animals should be killed, not even killing of the person who was responsible for the death of his beloved uncle. After many years of oppression, it was through peace, not war, that Muhammad gained sovereignty of Mecca. If we are going to take Muhammad's example, let's live as he did—according to the laws of the Koran.

ENDNOTES

Koran references are to the edition translated from Arabic to Persian by Mesbah Zadeh. Citations are *Chapter: Verse*; i.e. *2:17* means *Chapter Two, Verse Seventeen*. References to the Bible are the New King James version. For this book, "Torah" and "Old Testament" are interchangeable. "Bible" generally refers to the "New Testament."

PREFACE
1. 16:99.

INTRODUCTION
1. The Koran is written in Arabic, which can be read but not understood by Iranians, much as English speakers can read Spanish without understanding anything. Moslems are encouraged to read in Arabic rather than in their own language, with the assurance that this is more pious.

CHAPTER 1: THE HISTORY OF ISLAM
1. Gholamreza Saeid, Our Prophet's life, 1983, p. 46.
2. Gholamreza Saeid, Our Prophet's life, 1983, p. 54.
3. 4:3.
4. 4:(3,128).
5. "Imam" means "leader". Shiite Moslems think very highly of Ali and his eleven descendents, who are called the 12 imams.
6. 2:187, 214.

CHAPTER 2: THE THREE GREAT RELIGIONS
1. Although Moslems customarily refer to God as "Allah", they do not worship a separate God to Jews and Christians but the same one. "Allah" is just the Arabic word for God.
2. 23:(10-11).
3. 2:191, 4:33 and many more.
4. The Roman Catholic insistence on reading mass in Latin until after Vatican Two (1962-1965) is a close analogy with the current situation in Islam.

CHAPTER 3: THE LOSS OF ISLAM
1. 6:152-154.
2. Resalah of Khomeni, rule 2395.
3. 1:1, 2:19, 5:102, and many more.

4. 2:127.
5. 3:45, 5:111.
6. Resalah of Khomeni, rule 2826.
7. 41:34.
8. I Timothy, 3:1-12.
9. Luke, 11:45-50.
10. 6:156-158.
11. 3:2, 46:29.
12. 41:43, and many more, presented in section 9.2.
13. 5:18.
14. 5:22.
15. 2:254.
16. 3:37-41.
17. 3:52.

CHAPTER 4: THE RESALAH
1. The word "hadith" is used to indicate the singular; "ahadith" the plural.

CHAPTER 5: THE AHADITH—
THE ADULTERATION OF THE KORAN
1. 3:138, 46:8, 41:5, 29:17, and many more.
2. 3:126, 4:(62,71), 5:93, 47:35, 64:12.
3. 3:44.
4. 26:(108,126,131,144,150,163,179).
5. 5:18, 5:22, 5:52, 5:54, 5:71, 6:19, 6:50, 6:106
6. 6:130.
7. 26:(108,110).
8. 26:109-110.
9. 26:125-126.
10. 26:(127,131).
11. 26:150-151.
12. 26:161-163.
13. 17:47-51.
14. 2:181, 5:71, 6:(50,92), 7:(1-2,50,114-115,202), 10:1, 11:1, 12:1-4, 13:(1,37), 19:97, 20:(99,112), 21:(10,46,51), 25:(1,32), 26:1, 27:1-2, 32:1-2, 33:2, 36:69, 38:28, 45:5, 50:45, 57:9, 65:11, 69:44-48.
15. 3:138.
16. Mark, 7:8-9.
17. 12:111, 16:91.
18. 6:105.
19. 7:156.

20. 9:106.
21. 3:22, 5:71, 7:169, 45:27.
22. 3:87, 4:130, 5:(7, 71-72),6:156, 7:169, 45:(5-7).
23. 2:(183, 243), 3:22, 4:106, 7:(1-2), 18:26, 42:5, 57:9.
24. 27:78-79.

CHAPTER 6: WOMEN AND ISLAM

1. 4:38.
2. 4:39.
3. 4:127.
4. 4:12.
5. 4:4.
6. 2:233.
7. 2:233.
8. 5:(96, 105), 65:2.
9. 24:4.
10. 24:30-31.
11. 33:53.
12. 33:59.
13. 2:222.
14. 2:169.

CHAPTER 7: AMERICA AND ISLAM

1. 4:156, 6 (116,149), 10 (36,66), 33:10, 34:19, 37:85, 38:26, 41:(21,22,50), 45 (23,31), 48 (6,12), 72:7.
2. 49:12.
3. 2:28.
4. 2:29.
5. 2:30-31.
6. 2:30.

CHAPTER 8: HOLY WAR (JIHAD)

1. 4:97, 5:(39,59), 8:(73,75,76), 9:(16,19-20,24,41,44,74,80,82,87,89), 10:112, 22:77, 25:54, 47:33, 49:15, 61:11, 66:9.
2. 5:35.
3. 2:186.
4. Ironically, the closest analogy may be the Christian "crusade" against the Arab countries in the Middle Ages, when armies of Europeans slaughtered, plundered and raped their way through the Middle East in the name of God.

CHAPTER 9: JUDGE THE KORAN FOR YOURSELF

1. 44:58, 54:(17,22,32,40).
2. 33:32.
3. 2:1, 6:115, 7:50, 12:111, 16:91.
4. 5:52, 6:34, 7:202, 10:64, 18:26, 33:2.
5. "We", thus capitalized, refers to God.
6. 20:112, 12:1-2.
7. The house that was built by the prophet Abraham to symbolize the house of God.
8. 4:84, 18:1
9. 4:81, 8:55, 13:12.
10. The same message is also repeated in all the following verses of the Koran: 5:73, 7:40, 9:103, 10:(4,9), 11:(13,25), 13:28, 17:10, 18:(2,29,87,107), 28:(67,80), 29:(6,8,58), 34:(4,10,36), 35:8, 38:(23,27), 40:43, 41:7, 42:(21,22,25), 45:(14,20,29), 46:15, 47:(2,13), 48:29, 64:9, 65:11, 84:25, 95:6, 98:6, 103:3.
11. 2:59, 5:73.
12. Luke, 11:50-51.
13. Hardly surprising that Christ told the religious leaders of his day that their generation would be required of the blood of all the prophets.
14. 22:77.
15. 26:193-197, 41:43, 87:18-19.
16. Mark, 12:20-30.
17. 3:48.
18. 24:54 "If you believe in God and do good, you will be the rulers of the land, great ruling like the ruling like the one we gave to the ones before you." 3:132: "If you are a believer then you will be above all." Since in 3:48 we read that the followers of Jesus will be above non-believers, the inference clearly is that the scenarios envisioned in 3:132 and 24:54 will never come to pass. Moslems won't follow their book and be true believers.
19. Genesis, 18:23-32.
20. 3:(60-61).
21. John 6:38.

CHAPTER 10: THE TERRORISM OF SEPTEMBER 11TH, 2001

1. 49:12.
2. 2:160-162, 14:24-28.
3. 2:(233,286); 6:153; 7:40; 23:64; 65:7
4. This is discussed in detail in section 9.3.1.

CHAPTER 11: OVERLOOKED MESSAGES OF THE KORAN

1. 3:48.
2. 3:133.
3. 3:109-111.
4. Asfarol Arba-a, Volume 7, chapter 13, p. 136.
5. Abdul Karin Sharush, The Theory of Expanding and Shrinking, 1996, p. 82.

CHAPTER 12: GOD'S LAWS IN THE KORAN
vs. THE LAWS CREATED BY MAN

1. Almizan, chapter 6, pp. 14-16.
2. 2:1.
3. 2:9-10.
4. 10:37, 14:1, 18:52, 30:58, 39:28-29, 39:42, 40:37, 41:42, 47:(26-27), 50:45, 5:52.
5. Luke, 11:46.
6. 2:181, 5:9, 7:156.
7. Mark, 7:2-23.
8. 10:15, 13:21, 16:52, 17:59.
9. For example: 2:(104,172,277), 4:79, 5:(15,60), 9:(5,11,18,72), 19:(32,56), 21:73, 22:(42,77), 23:4, 24:(37,55), 27:3, 30:38, 31:3, 33:33, 41:6, 58:13, 73:20, 98:4.
10. See also 2:(2,192,216-8,255,263-267,269,271-275,277,280), 3:15, 4:38 and about 60 more.
11. 2:38-39, 56, 70, 73, 134, 141, 154-155, 164, 169-171, and many more (refer to section 9.5).
12. 33:56.
13. 58:9.
14. 3:57, 9:31.
15. 9:43; 33:37, 66:1.
16. 9:43.
17. 6:50, 7:156, 10:15.
18. 31:19-20, 31:5.
19. 7:29-30, 20:89-90.
20. 7:29-30, 16:14, 35:13.
21. 5:7.
22. 3:48.
23. Resalah of Khomeni, rules 6 and 7.
24. Almizan, Volume 1, p.64.
25. 2:59, 5:73.

26. 107:(2-7).
27. 28:54.
28. 6:143-144, 20:56, 22:(31,35), 39:8, 42:9.
29. 3:87-88, 6:151.
30. 2:167, 5:6.
31. 2:168.
32. Acts, 15:29.
33. Almizan, Volume I, Introduction.
34. Almizan, Volume I, Introduction.
35. 44:58; 54:(17,22,32,40).
36. Almizan, Volume I, Introduction.
37. Resalah of Khomeni, rule 105.
38. 18:17.
39. Resalah of Khomeni, rule 2615.
40. 5:97, 16:14, 35:13.
41. Resalah of Khomeni, rules 1272-1355.
42. 4:102.
43. Resalah of Khomeni, rule 1678.
44. Resalah of Khomeni, rules 2591-3.
45. 6:118-121.
46. 3:57, 9:31.
47. 72:19-23.
48. Luke, 11:15.

CONCLUDING NOTES
1. Matthew, 17:20.
2. 2:(44,116).
3. 4:44.
4. 4:157.
5. 10:47.
6. 45:27-30.
7. 107:1-7.